D0765140

NOT A COOKBOOK

A GUIDED JOURNEY TO COOKING WITHOUT RECIPES

MARGUERITE V. IMBERT

CONTENTS

NOT A
COOKBOOK

MARGUERITE V. IMBERT

INTRODUCTION

Most cookbooks focus on the **food**—specific dishes, ingredients, tools, timing and measurements.

Instead, this ~~cook~~book focuses on Y⊙U the cooking person.

It doesn't contain recipes. Instead, it helps you discover your **own**. ____

In this way, it's kind of like—**YOUR cookbook**.

It's my belief that you're a chef, whether you think of yourself as one or not. That all cooking emerges from human intuition. Every human—because of the sheer volume of times we interact with food— has preferences worth saving.

This book will help you record some of that knowledge, to make a record of this part of your identity, of who you are— from how you cook eggs, to how you grill and marinade, to how you choose ingredients, and what you eat for comfort.

I know that others want to know these bits from you too—which is why I encourage you to share what you learn along the way.

#NOTACOOKBOOK

Unlike most cookbooks, this book doesn't ask you to run out and buy any ingredients. Instead, it has you cook with what you already have.

It takes the premise that you have enough—so much—plenty! Think about your kitchen now—I'm sure it's FULL of so much stuff to cook.

Together, we'll experiment, write, breathe, stretch, and cook. As we go, I'll share my tips and tricks—the things that helped me to become a professional chef and—more importantly—the things that gave me the competence to cook for a lifetime ahead of me with ease and joy.

Let's get started. This is an 8-week journey of transformation, written by me (someone who made the transformation) **to** and **for** you.

GUIDELINES
FOR THE JOURNEY

Before we begin, let's agree on a few guidelines for our journey. First, what is a good cook?

It's different for everyone.

I have an atypical definition of a good cook, and it's one that I teach in this book. For me, being a good cook means being an unhindered one—it's a person who can cook anything they want without recipes.

To me, being a good cook is—a spirit and a feeling.

It's calmness, when a fire alarm goes off, when a pan starts to smoke a little too much, when a pot overboils.

It's joy, a feeling while you are in the kitchen that you are enjoying the space. It is giving you an outlet to be creative.

It's ease, making things quickly—without fuss—and naming them when they come out, not before.

It's confidence, knowing that you can do it—and allowing yourself to try making, say, spring rolls, even though you haven't made them before, and even if they turn out crazzzzy.

It's boldness and spontaneity, throwing a handful of pistachios into a grain bowl or battering lamb chops with pop rocks.

It's many more things to me, too, and I'll tell you more of those as we go through this book. Because to me, cooking well is an identity—one we'll foster here—as much as it's about the food we make.

What is a good cook to you?

Think of the qualities that come to mind. Each is in you.

Draw and write here.

To me, cooking well—cooking unhindered, with our senses, with our instinct (rather than other people's rules and prescriptions) is attainable for all of us.

Reflect again for a moment. Do you think everyone can be a good cook, or only some people? How about yourself? Are you included?

MANTRA
**as we journey, we agree to pursue the qualities
which we personally find compelling, and to be
open to the positive qualities that are beyond
our view.**

Who is this book for? This book is for everyone, for people of all ages and at all levels of cooking— from brand new to professional to anywhere in between. If you're a kid, I encourage you to ask a sibling, friend, cousin, or parent to join you in the process.

My way of cooking is not only my way of cooking. It's the ancient way, your ancestors' way, your way that's inside you. It's the senses coming together to create nourishment.

I cooked for many years while jotting down things I was learning or noticing. This book is the culmination of that time.

Throughout this book—you'll learn new things. New things I want you to know, and things that YOU want to know.

For example, have you often thought of learning how to make your own marshmallows? Or maybe you want to improve something—like how you make salmon? Write down these goals here. We'll come back to them later.

I'd like to learn

1.)

2.)

3.)

Now, do a little stretching and come back in a few.

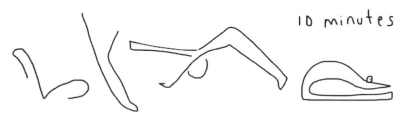

10 minutes

ARE YOU READY TO BEGIN?

WEEK 1 / DAY ONE

Assess your kitchen.

Welcome to the first day of this journey. I hope the impact of it will be felt in your life for years to come. Today, we're going to set the scene for a wonderful experience.

Since a lot of this experience will take place in your kitchen, let's head in there and do an assessment of the space.

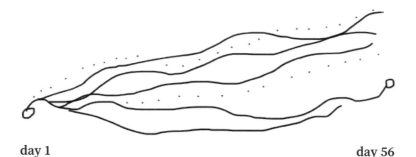

day 1   day 56

Most of us take loving care of our kitchens—and if I had to guess, I'd say you do too. But maybe there are some parts that could use improvement. Start by reflecting on these questions while you look at the space.

What are the dominant colors?

Is there a particular smell?

What does your kitchen sound like?

Any areas that you avoid?

Any areas you like more than others?

On the spectrum of messy to clean, how would you describe the state of your kitchen?

Write notes and draw pictures if you'd like.

We all have a way we want our kitchen to be, whether it's perky and fresh, or cozy and romantic. You may believe that spaces have a consciousness or want your kitchen to feel inviting to guests. Use this time together to take action on these visions that are inside you.

Do you have any thoughts about kitchens? Things you love or wish for yours?

Whatever state your kitchen is in, this first week together is about re-establishing your respect for and connection to this space.

Think of how often you and everyone else go into this space. So much movement, so much life. Kitchens are not meant to be museums—until we're gone—so for now, I don't want you to expect perfection, perfect cleanliness, perfect dishware, any of that.

This loving space is yours to use. And for you to enjoy cooking in it the most you can, I want to help you make it three things. Below each of these, add comments from your kitchen. How does it feel in each of these categories?

We want our kitchens to be hygienic, enlivening and functional.

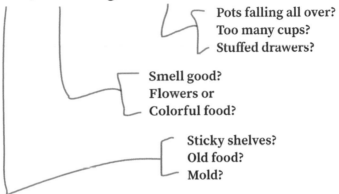

Pots falling all over?
Too many cups?
Stuffed drawers?

Smell good?
Flowers or
Colorful food?

Sticky shelves?
Old food?
Mold?

Let's go over each with regards to your space.

Hygienic—This week, we're going to take everything out, wipe surfaces down, and only put the good stuff back in. We want surfaces to be clean—not sticky from honey or sooty with coffee grounds. From your notes above, set up some actions below. Be specific and feel free to bullet point. How can your space improve in this way?

Enlivening—Our kitchens can inspire and uplift us. We can do this with color and light, as well as with bright scents and exciting foods. When I get fruit of almost any kind, I wash it in a colander and leave it on the counter on top of a hand towel.

When a holiday's approaching, I put something festive in a central location. Clipping a branch from your backyard and placing it at the center of your table brings this kind of simple enlivening vitality we all want and need.

 It's not about being fancy or doing it how other people do. It's about developing your own way of bringing life and vitality into your space. Put some action items below for the week ahead. Even just the act of writing something down plants a seed we can keep watering. How can your space improve in this way?

Functional—Your kitchen should work well for you. Morning things should be in a convenient place for you to enjoy using when you're still tired, for instance.

While some people think of bringing in new tools, clearing objects out is often the best way to make a kitchen more functional. If you have twenty glasses, consider donating ten. If you have repeats, like three can openers instead of one, get down to one.

With groceries, think of buying food only when there's not a lot in your kitchen already. Too much food becomes a source of disfunction, even though it's intended to help.

Are any cabinets or drawers stuffed or hard to navigate? Write them down here. How can your space improve in this way?

Now, let's decide on what areas need to get cleaned. Take your time filling out this chart as you scan your kitchen.

(Think about all the major sections of your kitchen first— your fridge, your snack cabinets—as well as the little sections—your utensil drawer, the pen drawer, the dog food area, section where you place your kitchen towels, etc.)

Feel free to cut this chart out and tape it to your fridge.

Tomorrow, we'll go through it, checking off boxes as you go.

I'd like you to go about this entire process intuitively. If it takes you longer to get through this entire chart, let that be okay. Maybe you tackle a section a day for as many days in a row as you can.

Start thinking about your plan tonight, and tomorrow we'll set our WOOP—I'll explain what that means in the morning!

WEEK 1 / DAY TWO
Clean your kitchen.

Now that you have your chart filled out, let's set up your time frame. For stragglers, go fill out that chart now! It's not too late—we'll wait.

To set up your time frame for cleaning, let's use a motivational tool I like. It's called WOOP. It goes like this: **Wish, Outcome, Obstacles, and Plan.**

Name your **wish**. Let's say it's "clean every section in the chart today."

Next, name the **outcome** (what's the value for you in accomplishing that.) Maybe it's "a feeling of starting fresh" or "the ability to love one of my spaces so much more."

Now, write the **obstacles** to achieving the wish (what could get in your way?). For me it's often "getting distracted by other things." What's it for you?

Next, we set up a **plan** to overcome those specific

obstacles. Yours could be "make a big pot of coffee to drink throughout the cleaning session and let myself drink as often as I want." Or, for a more holistic example, "turn my phone off and stick to my kitchen and my cleaning."

Fill out your kitchen cleaning WOOP here. Be realistic as well as excited to surprise yourself—you can always create mini WOOPs as you go today. Example: "my wish for the next hour is…"

Wish -

Outcome -

Obstacle -

Plan -

Now, clean the sections in your chart. For each section, take all the objects out and wipe down the surfaces of the section.

If objects like honey containers or protein powders are sticky, wash or wipe them down before putting them back in their section.

Once you're done with your WOOP for today, sit down in your kitchen or nearby and enjoy your progress.

What do you **love** about your kitchen that you noticed today as you cleaned? Let's appreciate its sweet details—

draw your favorite
of its features

♡ favorite part

(circle one or two)

faucet   walls   fridge

vibe a tool the layout

cozy personal busy

What about your kitchen is special to you? Kind of—magical or awesome?

It's that it it's _____.

As a private chef, I cooked in ALL kinds of kitchens—big, small, old, new, for single people, big families, homes full of housemates, new parents, nursing moms—and I've loved each and every one. (ESPECIALLY after we did some cleaning and organization.)

For the rest of the day, take time to enjoy and appreciate your kitchen. Every part of it—and its ability to change and grow, like you.

You're doing great! Tomorrow, we'll go over your inventory.

WEEK 1 / DAY THREE
Review your tools.

Today, we'll go section by section through your kitchen tools. We'll affirm the value of what you have and make changes where needed, whether that means donating tools or buying new tools.

MANTRA
i love and affirm all the wonderful tools in my life.
i release what i don't use, so others can find
extraordinary value in what I don't need.

Prepare a box or bag. In most neighborhoods, putting a box of things on the street is a great way to bring joy and serendipity to others. If letting go of things makes you nervous, plan to move some things to a storage room or closet in your home.

Plan to let go of what you don't use. In order to most benefit from this moment together, plan to move things OUT of the kitchen space. Can you commit to that? Let's do it together.

These are my thoughts on what you need. Add

your own as we go in the margins.

Check each of these categories, and downsize where needed. As you count and hold the things you have, you imbed them with conscious cooperation. As you move things out that don't get used, you are opening space for creativity and flow.

Plates, bowls, utensils and glasses: Many people have too many of these things. Very rarely will more than ten big plates be practical in a home, for instance. You can have them as backup, but consider having only ten max in your kitchen itself.

Pots and pans: Chances are you have a lot of pots and pans, too. Go through your stash and prepare to reduce. If you have a pot that often burns or feels too heavy on your wrist, donate. They'll be perfect for someone else.

I need three pots: small, medium and large. Any more and I feel like the section is overflowing.

For pans, I like a large cast iron skillet and a large non-stick skillet, then a few small non-stick skillets for smaller projects (and, as bonus, maybe a small cast iron skillet).

If you have—a cast iron skillet and a non-stick pan—you're good.

Lodge, 9-inch, seasoned   **A lightweight one**

Any that you love? Thoughts on your collection? (Write or draw them here.)

Now, let's look at your Tupperware. You don't need to have Tupperware per se, but you will want to have containers of some kind (glass jars or plastic take-out food containers are just as good as my favorite—Pyrex with snap lids.)

Today, let's pair lids and keep only those containers with lids. Ditch any that are broken. Lastly, run containers through the dishwasher that need it. If you know you need a new set, order a two dozen pack of mason jars or Pyrex with snap lids.

Cabinet organization. Many kitchens don't have any kind of official organizing system in the cabinets, and that's fine. A lot of containers that foods come in are good enough.

What I suggest is having a set of containers that you can use as an option when you want to—say for plastic bags of oats, or loose candy.

If you have unused jars and tubs in your Tupperware section, use them for loose ends in your cabinets. Go at this today.

Focus on making things convenient for yourself. If your morning breakfast is oats with hot kettle water and chocolate chips, brown sugar, maca powder, hemp seeds and chia seeds—get those items in little jars rather than having to reach into heavy bags all the time.

MANTRA
i create ease and balance in my space.
my instinct is strong—it tells me what i like.
i love to be organized. it's in my nature.

I hope today will be INSPIRING as you make these changes—what's amazing about a home owner getting into organization mode is how much CREATIVITY comes out. Let yourself flow.

Blender and food processor. All working blenders are very helpful to us as cooks, and we'll use them together through the journey. If you're looking for the best option, look into a Vitamix (gets everything the smoothest.)

In terms of food processors, KitchenAids and Cuisinarts of all models are reliable in my experience. If splurging or setting an alert on

Craigslist, the Robot Coupe is a restaurant-quality food processor that's super strong and won't overheat, no matter how much you make. Again, whatever food processor you have—awesome.

Don't have either? I recommend you order one or the other today. If you're doubtful you'll use them, pause. Think on it as you continue through the journey.

Now for mixing bowls. If you're stocking a kitchen for the first time or want to start fresh, nesting bowls are ideal because they stack perfectly on top of each other and give the kitchen a consistent look. I like the look and feel of aluminum or stainless steel more than plastic or Pyrex ones.

Today, notice and count the bowls that you consider mixing bowls. If you don't have any bowls you feel are mixing bowls, this is a gentle, loving reminder to stock up in this category. Order a set of three aluminum nesting bowls for your new kitchen life.

i love taking care of myself.
i love giving myself what i need to thrive and grow.
i always know what i need, and i know when it's the
right time to take care of myself in a new way.

Knives. Take stock of your knives—from butter knives to your sharpest ones. Kids, get an adult to help you with this step. Here's the list of my essentials:

1) **A 6-8'-inch chef's knife.** I prefer closer to six because I find I get a better handle on it.

2) **A long serrated knife**, ideal for cutting crusty loaves of bread and pineapples.

3) **A few smaller serrated knives** for cutting juicy tomatoes or other foods with delicate skin that need grip.

4) **Paring knives** to cut strawberries or devein shrimp (devein = remove the thin black string that runs down the back of raw shrimp that is actually, fun fact, their digestive system)

5) **Butter knives** for butter, jam and other gentle things.

I'm guessing you have a lot of knives. So, for most of you, this is an invitation to sort through your knives and donate the ones you don't like (often these are the ones we ignore.)

Remember when you donate to follow precautions—wrap in bubble wrap, put in a bag, and label. You don't want anyone cutting themselves, and for those of you who are putting things on the street—I'm no officer, but I would say, don't put knives on the street, okay?

Cutting boards. I think of cutting boards and pans as our canvases—the backdrop to our food, like plates. Today, check yours and see if you want to upgrade.

I like wood or bamboo cutting boards made out of a single piece of wood (when they're made out of several pieces, I've had snaps.) I like plastic cutting boards too because they're lightweight, flexible, and can go in the dishwasher. Adjust your collection.

MANTRA
i am creating a kitchen
that is conducive to art and creativity.
i am drawn to uplifting energy and materials.

Accessories. Finally, let's talk about accessories.
Use this space to sort through what you have and
what you need.

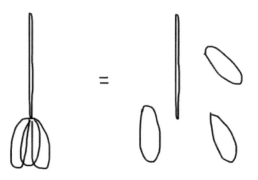

Funny or poignant stories that involve my kitchen
utensils or accessories:

It's nice to have a whisk, for sure, and most
kitchens already do, but I use a fork for a lot of stuff
even if I have a whisk in a drawer (like for whisking
eggs).

I don't feel I need a peeler (I just rinse my carrots well, and keep the skin on when I mash potatoes). I don't find I need a lemon squeezer or a garlic mincer, either (although I squeeze lemons with a fork every morning and I do find myself avoiding garlic just generally—cumbersome even with the mincer.)

What do you love or need in terms of kitchen items? Use this space to organize your thoughts.

About Crocks

I recommend a crock next to your stove with your favorite cooking utensils in it. Key here is favorite. Many of you have crocks and they're overfilled. For those with cooking utensils in a drawer, repurpose a flower vase.

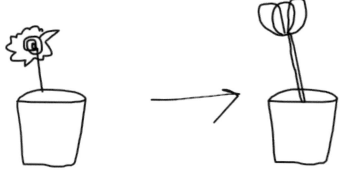

Write a joke caption for the image above.

Overall, with kitchen accessories, I find less is more.

Make sure you have a can opener. If you're buying a can opener for the first time, get one with covered handles for comfort. Kitchen scissors are also great for cutting packages open, slicing fish, and it's awesome you can clean most in the dishwasher.

Taking stock of what you have—That was the point of today. Did you do that? Even just in a few major sections? Good. If not, pause. Go back and do today's section again tomorrow.

Next, we'll organize the contents of your fridge—whatever's in there is great. You can look forward to it—it will be fun! Sleep well and see you then.

WEEK 1 / DAY FOUR
Enter your fridge.

As a private chef, the first and last thing I did during sessions was organize the fridge. When I arrived, I'd consolidate bottles of things (olives, milks) and take out anything that was almost done and I could use as a start for cooking.

At the end, I'd do what we'll do below. Think balance, ease, and space. For all of us, the fridge is a scene we're returning to again and again. It's a beautiful place.

Today, we'll care for it.

Start by opening your fridge. What do you see? Write it here, and express any changes you'd like to experience.

If you had to roast your fridge, comedy style, what you say? For example: my fridge is so _____ a _____ could _____ in it.

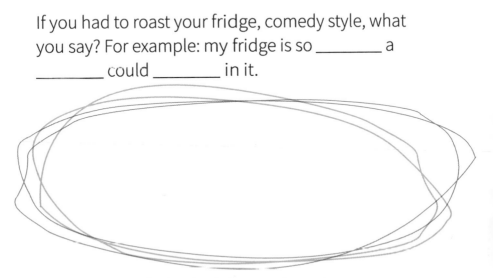

However your fridge is doing, we're going to improve it today. Let's get in there.

Think about your sections. What goes on top and what goes on the bottom? In the door, or in the butter container? Organize your thoughts here.

Now, from front to back, bring things closer to you that you use more often. Is something you use often out of reach? Adjust.

Is anything stuffed? If your vegetable drawer barely opens when you pull it open, pull it out and go through the contents. In a functional fridge, we want all of the drawers to glide easily in and out.

Is there a crowded sense? Scan the main shelves and the door to the fridge. Consolidate containers and minimize where you can. When things are too crowded, you have spills and frustration. We want all objects to move easily in relation to each other.

Anything beautiful hiding out? An example of this would be a bag of cherries in a brown paper bag, stuffed in a vegetable drawer. Take out the rare and beautiful unicorns of your fridge and display them on your counter. Peaches, cherry tomatoes, peppers, and apples. What other beautiful things would you love to see on your counters? What are the most beautiful fruits according to your discerning eyes?

For final touches, think of Tetris. Orient objects so they're about parallel to each other, with some healthy space in between. If you find leftovers in shoddy (not totally secure) containers, transfer them to better containers now. Move small amounts of things that are in large containers to smaller containers. Once the fridge feels good, take a deep breath and shut the door.

Tomorrow, we'll move on to your freezer. I hope you're enjoying your beautiful fridge. See you soon!

WEEK 1 / DAY FIVE
Organize your freezer.

Today, let's dive into your freezer, one of my favorite parts of a kitchen. None of us go into it TOO often, but when we do—it's for like, ice cubes, mochi balls, or frozen pizza.

Silence. "Far out."

That's what your freezer is, folks—far out! To get back in touch with it, we're getting in there.

I think of the freezer like a time capsule. It keeps things fresh so we can take them out later. If you get a dozen donuts as a gift, you can freeze half of them right away, and take the pressure off yourself to eat them quickly.

MANTRA
i am connected to my ancestors through my freezer.
this wise part of my life lets me save things of value
for when i need them. i take my time.
i have reverence and love for those before me.

OK this section is making me cold. Let's move quickly!

When to freeze: You want to freeze things while they're fresh. If something's possibly moldy or has started to go bad, don't freeze it. Today, look around your kitchen and see what you could proactively freeze to use later. (Record here.)

What freezes well? Almost every hot dish (soups and things), cooked rice (or any other grains), hummus, sticks of butter, breads and bagels, pastries of all kinds (cake and donuts), fruit (if you really think you can't eat it fresh, best is to chop first to use later in smoothies), sauces, meats and fish of all kinds that are not yet cooked.

What do you like to freeze? Any debates among family members?

What doesn't freeze well? Most raw vegetables (lettuce or carrots, for instance.) My personal exceptions to this are dark greens like, say, kale or spinach.

If I'm heading out on a trip and there's a big head or two left of kale in the fridge, I might just throw them both in the freezer (do wrap, or you get bits on the bottom of the freezer.) I'd use them later for smoothies or maybe a soup (but I wouldn't try using them for a side dish—and definitely not as a salad.)

What's just OK to freeze? Things like fried rice. Thoughts to add?

Ok, let's get that freezer cleaned.

Take everything out of your freezer and start to put together an organizational plan for the space.

Now, let me say this: Very few people have an organized fridge, but you'll feel great if yours is. It doesn't take much effort but it makes a difference.

Often with the freezer it's more like abstract categories ('on the left', 'smoothie stuff;' 'on the right,' 'vegetables and things.')

Many freezers are packed. Let's do some clearing. Remove ice packs you don't use and random things you don't want in there.

When your freezer feels refreshed, you're done!

Tomorrow we'll talk grocery shopping. If you're following this process, you've done a lot of clearing. I'm not going to ignore your progress even for a second. What is this corresponding to in your life? Write about what this new energy means to you here.

WEEK 1 / DAY SIX
Reform how you shop.

When I first started cooking, I'd get cookbooks from the public library and fill them with post-it notes. I'd make lists of ingredients and bring them to the grocery shop with a pen in hand, crossing things off on my list as I went. "Do you have spirulina? Do you know where the bread crumbs are?"

If I hit a dead end with one ingredient, it'd be like, "Okay, I guess I don't need this, this, this or THIS anymore. Were those jars of cherries for the next recipe? Or was it that pie that need condensed milk? I can't remember!"

If you shop based on recipes, you might relate. If you shop ad hoc but generally feel overwhelmed or confused about grocery shopping, or just sort of blah, we're going to fix that all up today.

Let's start with: **Where You Go.**

If you HATE grocery shopping, I hear you. You're probably either: 1) really busy or 2) in a small and perfectly honorable category of people who really don't like it. This was one of the first things I determined with clients (I did not grocery shop for the majority of them).

Any of them who did not like grocery shopping— and after I was like "THAT'S OKAY"—I'd ask them to get on Imperfect Foods or Instacart, or in some cases join a CSA (where you get produce mailed to your house, but in my experience, more often need to pick it up.)

If you like your grocery shopping experience, let's feel into that. First off, where do you go? How does each place make you feel? Imagine being in that space. Name the place, then how it feels for you.

1

2

3

4
5
6

You might find that some of your stops foster RELATIONSHIPS, others feel ASPIRATIONAL or INSPIRE YOU to discover new foods.

(And maybe some of them stress you out. Go ahead and cross out those stressful ones.)

Our main grocery stores should be places we look forward to going into, even if they're virtual. Consider where you go and if you want to change your system in any way.

Write some suggestions to yourself here:

What You Buy

When you cook without recipes, grocery shopping will be different than if you shop based on recipes. With the system we'll use on this journey—you can shop intuitively—based on what your body is asking for and what you know is wholesome for yourself in general.

If this feels new, be gentle with yourself.

MANTRA
i thrive on variety and color.
i follow my instinct.
i eat what i need to feel happy and well.

Today—in preparation for shopping tomorrow—we'll explore some of the foods that put you at your best. Grocery shopping is the time when we choose the foods that become the quality of our lives.

To me, grocery shopping involves two parts:

1. Foods and drinks **that have become fixtures in my life based on their impact**. This category needs a little thought, so we'll spend today exploring it.

2. Foods and drinks **I choose in response to how I'm doing**— in the week or so before shopping, considering the season, mood and energy levels.

HOW TO KNOW WHAT TO EAT

There are many traditions—Ayurveda, traditional Chinese Medicine, herbalism, the list goes on—that guide us to choose food based on our constitution as well as our more fluctuating states.

But there's nothing better than **your own body's instinct**.

When I was living in France in a farmhouse with chickens and not much more but a river and a medieval town nearby—I got to the point of sickness with regards to food. So much wine, bread, cheese, chocolate. I've been there many times in life—where the dose or combinations of foods become an opponent, bringing poor health rather than strong health.

A simple exercise came to me that, having only done it once, changed my life forever. I wrote down the first food that came to mind, followed by whatever immediate reaction or feeling that came to me directly after naming it.

Name as many foods as you can, followed by the feeling you get when you think of that food.

Use this diagram below to chart the foods that make you feel GREAT on the left. On the right, name some foods that feel less helpful to you or make you itchy / tired / or any other negative feelings.

Let's use this left side as a basis for your shopping tomorrow. If you still need more support revising this aspect of your life, here's a little bit about how I shop, which I do consider to be exemplary, ehem, ehem.

48

How I Shop

In general, I choose nutrient-dense foods over nutrient-poor ones (so kale over iceberg lettuce), colorful foods over pale ones (purple tomatoes over white potatoes), diversity and exposure over sameness (and, as a result, multitude over volume), minimum waste over standard waste (jars over plastic bags).

We're all different. What general principles come to mind for your way of shopping?

Tomorrow, you'll go grocery shopping using some of what you mused on today.

We'll talk first, so I'll see you then!

WEEK 1 / DAY SEVEN
Grocery shopping.

Good morning! It's grocery shopping day. If you feel all set—great. If you need a little more help—read through this grocery list and cross out anything you intuitively don't want.

If you live in a household with others, this is a good opportunity to invite them to sit alongside you as you go through it and discuss.

MANTRA
i love treating my body with love.
i feed it great foods, good thoughts
and anything else it needs to thrive.

Here is the exact list I used to send to all of my clients before coming into their homes for the first time—with the preface to "exclude anything you don't like, and add anything that catches your eye."

(This list would be edited for allergies. For instance, I'll remove grains if there's a grain allergy in the family, and so on.)

For the produce section, I'd list produce that was locally in season. Farmer's markets cut out that step because they won't feature things not grown locally. For my families who shopped at the farmers market, I'd tell them to choose whatever produce catches their eye. Our eyes are the first part of the digestive system!

Sample Grocery List

GRAINS & LEGUMES: Basmati rice, black rice, barley, quinoa, sorghum, oats, farro, wheatberries, black or green lentils, and a mix of gluten free or whole wheat pastas if you like!

NUTS & SEEDS: Raw slivered almonds, whole almonds, cashews, pecans, walnuts, sunflower seeds, pine nuts, hemp seeds, chia seeds

PRODUCE: Fresh herbs: parsley, cilantro, basil, rosemary, sage, thyme, dill, and oregano. The produce that last longest are apples, pears, cabbage, squashes, potatoes and other root vegetables. Try and get some of your favorite leafy greens and lettuces (collards, spinach, kale, arugula, cabbage), and some of the following: brussels sprouts, stone fruits, leeks, tomatoes, corn, shallots, scallions, ginger, parsley, lemons, cucumbers, cauliflower, yellow and purple onions, red bell peppers, parsley, and basil. I love prewashed veggies too—get any you like.

FROZEN STUFF: Corn, peas, edamame, berries

ADDITIONAL BASICS: Dijon mustard, extra virgin olive oil, coconut oil, one or two of the hearty oils (don't go for vegetable oil, instead take a couple specific oils like avocado oil, grapeseed, or sunflower), red and white wine vinegars, sherry vinegar, apple cider vinegar, balsamic vinegar and rice vinegar, canned tomato paste (a little goes a long way), canned coconut cream, canned tomatoes, almond butter, agave nectar, honey, cranberries, golden raisins, currants, canned chickpeas, miso paste, tahini, tamari or liquid amino acids, capers

SPICES: Red pepper flakes, curry powder, cumin, cayenne, smoked paprika, ground ginger, and cinnamon. Don't bother buying the following dried / always go for the fresh version: rosemary, dill, thyme, sage, oregano, tarragon

CHEESE: Fresh shredded parmesan, crumbled blue cheese, feta cheese, mozzarella balls, and anything else that you like! I like aged and hardened cheeses, which are lower in lactose. Vegan cheeses are great too. Try one!

PROTEIN: Whole eggs; wild fish (salmon, black cod, mahi mahi, grouper, herring, trout, or anything else that you like), frozen wild shrimp; grass-fed chicken, grass-fed beef if you like it, bone broth if you'd like.

Enjoy your shopping today and I'll see you tomorrow. During week two, we'll start edging into cooking and using the beautiful space you prepared this week.

MANTRA
i love feeling prepared.
i am surrounded by abundance and possibility.

WEEK TWO

LET'S GET COOKING!
WE START SLOWLY BUT
SURELY THIS WEEK.

Every day includes an active cooking exercise.
We'll explore a concept or practice a new
approach.

Coming at it in a new way

Let's start the week with a WOOP. Your wish for
this week with regards to your cooking and this
journey—

Wish -
Outcome -
Obstacles -
Plan -

WEEK 2 / DAY ONE
Explore one ingredient.

Today, go into your kitchen and find a food item (like sauerkraut) or an ingredient (like cumin) that you only know a little about—there should be plenty like this.

Next, Google it, letting yourself wander through the results. When you're done, close the device and write down a definition for the item here.

Now, have your own experience with it.

> **How does it smell?**
> **Look?**
> **Taste?**
> **What would go well with it?**

Head back into your kitchen and combine or arrange this item with something else—for the purpose of eating. Mix it up, apply heat, do whatever you want and whatever feels intuitive.

56

No recipe! Once you've finished, read this passage.

One of the things we'll practice together is naming dishes that you make.

One of the differences between a chef and not a chef is that chefs regularly name the food they make!

Names also matter to our eaters—they help us manage their expectations. Names should be clear, accurate and—when appropriate—engaging, funny or exciting. But accuracy is the most important part of naming dishes.

Imagine someone giving you a piece of chocolate cake and calling it a 'brownie' versus calling it 'chocolate cake.' In the first situation, you'd be like, 'huh!" In the second, voila—peace and wonder.

As you're cooking, and especially when you're tasting—think—what will I name this?

Good job completing your challenge today. Can you name what you made today?

Tomorrow, we'll play with a fundamental concept—heat!

WEEK 2 / DAY TWO
Explore heat.

Hot and cold—they're so fundamental—concepts that belong to all of us, are felt by all of us. My point is—no one knows heat better than you. You're alive. And in a big way—

Cooking is about managing

In kitchens, we often use heat to cook in three ways. Read these ways out loud, slowly and deliberately. Debate with someone near you as needed:

1. the oven, which cooks food using indirect heat, through hot air touching the food.

2. a pan, which cooks food through direct heat, by contacting the food with a hot surface

3. a pot, which cooks food by immersing it directly in hot liquid

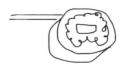

So, this week, when you're looking at something you want to cook, think—which of these three ways will I use?

You could bake something in the oven, cook something in a pan, or boil something in a pot. It's simple. All methods work.

Let's take a potato, for instance. You could boil it. You could sit it on an oven rack and let it bake. Or you could chop it up and put it in a pan. You can cook that potato ANY of these three ways—and that's just the beginning.

Why do you need to chop it up if you use the pan? Because you're relying on that surface heat. So by chopping, you're getting more of its surface area down on the heat.

Because we're using heat today, I quickly want to talk about **safety**! There's one trick I use to avoid burns in the kitchen, which has become a regular part of my cooking routine.

When I'm cooking in a kitchen with a lot of different dishes going on, both hot and cold—I tap all surfaces that are potentially hot quickly before taking a more committed grip. This is much better than grasping something hot with a full grip.

Any tips for avoiding burns? Burns you remember?

Write some of your own cooking safety tips here. Ask your crew for theirs.

Today we'll focus on the first method: pans.

Pans cook things unevenly, and that's one of their superpowers.

If something's cooking on a hot surface, whatever side is closest to the surface will cook the most. In the case of chicken, the side facing down gets browned, while the top part stays pale.

If you're brand new to pans, try this order:

1) Decide whether you need or want to chop what you're cooking. This depends a lot on the heartiness and size of the vegetable. Raw cherry tomatoes? Sure. Whole raw carrots? Probably not.

2) Place the pan on the burner, turn on the heat, and add an oil, butter or ghee.   ghee = Clarified butter

Try to get the food dry first before adding it to the pan—extra water will slow the cooking.

3) Add the food to the pan. Observe. Adjust when you feel the instinct. If you want something to brown, try to leave it alone for a bit.

My favorite cooking oil is avocado oil. Yours?

If your pan starts to smoke, turn the overhead fan on and move the pan to another burner that's off. You have control over this heat. Adjusting is awesome. Listen, stay, and observe.

Another option for an overly hot pan is to throw in a handful of, say, kale or spinach. It will cool off the pan, cook quickly, and act like a sponge for all the bits off the pan's surface—usually tasty stuff.

If you're cooking on a cast iron skillet, remember you can put it into the oven too. Brown your food on the stove, then transfer it to the oven to cook more slowly —if you want. It gets it out of your way.

Relish in your ability to adjust and take care of what's here.

let's get cooking.

Pick one of your pans to cook with today! Draw it here.

Now—to decide what to cook with it, browse your kitchen for two categories:

1. **WHAT YOU HAVE A LOT OF**
2. **WHAT COULD SOON GO BAD**

Look for a starting point within one of those two categories. Then, use your pan to cook what you chose. Incorporate anything I've told you and write any of your own insights here. What did you cook?

Last thing for today: Once you've finished cooking and removed the food from the pan, I want you to use the residual heat (notice how that pan's still hot) to toast a piece of bread or brown some almonds or warm up some grains from the fridge.

As we journey together,

Think about using all heat you create

Heat is valuable. Not just the amount of heat that can turn a chicken edible, but also the smaller more subtle lingering heat.

How can we honor leftover heat? I'll write three and you add two.

1) LEAVE THE OVEN DOOR OPEN AFTER BAKING TO WARM THE HOUSE.

2) POUR HOT (CLEAN) POT WATER ON TOP OF MUGS, BEFORE USING THEM FOR COFFEE, TO WARM THEM UP.

3) POUR HOT POT WATER ONTO STICKY PANS OR DISHES SITTING IN THE SINK, RATHER THAN THROWING IT DIRECTLY DOWN THE DRAIN.

4)

5)

Great job today. I'll see you tomorrow.

WEEK 2 / DAY THREE
Boil something.

Hello! Did you cook without setting the fire alarm off yesterday? That's awesome. I'm proud of you.

But don't be scared if it DOES go off. They can go off for all kinds of earnest reasons, like too much cooking happening in a kitchen at once or being in a space that's small. It's not always because you're doing something silly, but, hey, sometimes that's the case too.

Either way, as long as we're fire free, we're all good!

Good cooks like YOU know how to handle a fire alarm. It's one of the little details that sets you apart. Other people will freak out, but you won't. Here's what we do instead if that happens.

First off, stay calm. Then, stand on a chair to touch the main button of the fire alarm until it turns off. Hold it down longer if it doesn't turn off after a single tap.

Next, open the windows, doors if you can, and set the culprit pan outside (when possible, if there's a backyard or balcony.) Wave the air toward the open door or window with a dish towel. If the alarm goes off again, get back on that chair.

Within minutes, you can get back to cooking. Once you're cooking again, be mindful of the source of the issue, and aim to go low on heat for a bit (pans are most likely of the three cooking methods to set the alarm off.)

(It happens.)

ALRIGHT, now that we covered that important topic, let's move on to talk about **pots**: the second method of cooking with heat. Select a pot and let's get ready to use it.

Most often we use pots to boil food, so let's boil something today. Whenever you're boiling, you don't need to measure the water you use. Fill the pot up from the tap, and put it on the burner. When you add what you're going to boil, make sure it is fully immersed in the water.

FAST BOILING-ELECTRIC KETTLES

When I'm about to boil something—pasta or potatoes, for instance—my preference is to start with my electric kettle. It's quicker to pour hot water from the kettle into a pot rather than boiling straight from the stove, start to end. No kettle? Start from the pot on the stove. I do that a lot of times too, especially if I have the time.

Alright, now what to boil today? Look at all your hearty vegetables. Pick one! There are a number of reasons I love boiling vegetables, even though roasting is much more in fashion and allows you to get more color and texture. I do both! Why boil?

1) **You don't have to cut the vegetables up that much.** For example, I like to put a whole cauliflower down into a boiling pot of water, or cut it in half if it's big. (Remember— whole things need to be immersed for them to cook evenly.)

2) **You don't need fat.** Vegetables would dry out and stick to the pan if you cooked them on a pan or in the oven without a fat, but boiling in a pot, no problem: they stay nice and hydrated just with water. Because fats are among the pricier things we buy per ounce, boiling is economical.

3) **It's immersive heat.** This means things cook faster. To feel the extent of this, throw a big handful of spinach into a

simmering pot of stew and enjoy how quickly it cooks down. You could get a whole bag of spinach that would fill your biggest salad bowl raw to cook down into a soup in seconds. In other words, it delivers and is strong.

To salt the water or not? My experience says it's really up to you. I almost always salt the boiling water when I'm making pasta (less if it's fresh pasta). I only sometimes salt with potatoes. Like I started to say in point #2, you don't need seasoning with boiling and that's great.

That said, a boiling vegetable like a carrot will rarely complain if you decide to generously enhance the water—with butter, salt, sugar, a whole garlic clove, whatever. (Just remember if you DO take this route to really clean the vegetable first and plan to reuse the fortified liquid afterward.)

Any tips for salting or not salting your water that you want to record?

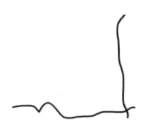

When do you use lids? A lid will trap heat and make the situation in your pot hotter. I put a lid on a pot if I need something to cook faster, like if beans are taking a long time to soften or to encourage pasta water to boil faster (I'll sometimes start with the lid on).

How do you know when food is done? Use a butter knife. When it slides to the center of the vegetable, the vegetable is cooked. If it still feels hard, let it continue boiling.

How do you know if you over-boil? If you can mash what you cooked once it comes out. But mashing is great (go with it + add butter)!

If you overboil and you want the thing to perform as if you didn't, you can reverse time a bit by pouring the food into a colander and rinsing it thoroughly under cold water. It will stop the cooking process and wash the excess starch from the outsides.

(I love rinsing grains or pastas if they overcook.)

What did you boil today? What did you learn?

Tomorrow, we'll continue cooking with pots.
Sleep well and see you then!

WEEK 2 / DAY FOUR
Awaken cooking intuition.

Let's start with a breathing exercise today. I taught this one a lot as a yoga and meditation teacher. I think of it as an adaptogenic breath exercise, because it seems to work well with many energetic states, sort of elevating or more so evolving whatever state you're in.

Inhale through your nose for 5 counts.

Hold your breath for 7 counts.

Exhale out your mouth for 8 counts.

↳ Inhale 5, hold 7, exhale 8. 👄

through nose   through mouth

Repeat that three times.

Did you feel a subtle change? Write about it here.

What's an adaptogen? It's a substance that adapts based on the condition it enters: for one person, it lifts. For another, it calms, tonifies, solidifies, or any other number of affects. It works WITH you—meeting your system in a way that might be different to a person next to you. Popular examples are herbs like ashwagandha, rhodiola, astragalus, and mushrooms like reishi or cordyceps.

They help your body to adapt—to stress, to changing times, to new circumstances. On this journey together, you'll show up in all kinds of moods and energy levels. How are you today?

Today, as you cook, return to the 5-7-8 breathing exercise throughout your time. Let your mind and body guide you to a food or drink that is helpful to your current state. Name a few connections from your experience.

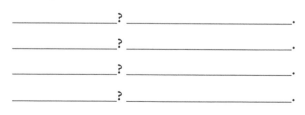

One of my go-tos for feeling uneasy is hibiscus tea, or if I'm ungrounded I'll go for hot turmeric milk, or ashwagandha with milk and honey in the evening.

Most kitchen substances can be soothing and healing—can assist us in adapting to current circumstances—if we are led to them intuitively.

Head into your kitchen and explore from this frame of mind. Write down what you prepared and any feelings you are supporting through your creativity with food or drink today.

WEEK 2 / DAY FIVE
Incorporate labeling.

Today, let's talk labeling. The simplest, chicest, most affordable way to make your fridge feel special. I like a black sharpie and either Avery labels, masking tape or post-its.

I prefer to use real labels for things like DIY house spray (we'll make some together soon), and post-it notes for short-term things (like, 'onion' when you put half an onion into an opaque yogurt tub).

MANTRA
i am honored by the things in my life. i came here with a special mission to thrive and connect.

Today, prepare your labeling options, then open your fridge and begin labeling. This is an exercise of adding language to your fridge—instantly making it more dynamic and compelling, as well as easier.

As you label things in your fridge, allow your mind to wander through the possibilities: why label this, why not this. This exercise will attach your natural desire to organize with the act of looking at your fridge—a space you look at a lot.

What to label? What not to label?

Clear Tupperware of chopped pineapple—don't label. White Chinese food carton—transfer to a clear container, and label 'brown rice' with a post-it.

Any organization tips you want to add? What qualities that are within you does your refrigerator reflect today?

WEEK 2 / DAY SIX
Simmer something loose.

Today we'll cook again with a pot. Instead of boiling, we'll simmer. Simmering is less aggressive than boiling. It's smaller bubbles and it's more of a slow cooking approach.

 SIMMERING ‹ BOILING

The reason I say 'loose things' is because I cook most loose things the same—and I want you to recognize that you can, too. I mean rice, beans, quinoa, all of it.

A lot of people have specific ways of cooking rice. My grandmother Mimi—a Frenchwoman based in New Orleans with five children—cooked a lot of rice.

She used 2 cups water to 1 cup rice. She would bring the water to a boil first with a chicken bouillon cube dissolved in it. Then, she put in the rice and added ¼ cup of chopped parsley on top of the water. She'd cover the pot and turn the fire low, simmering for 20 minutes. Afterwards, she'd fluff with a fork and serve. If she didn't use the bouillon, instead she'd put a pad of butter on top of the rice before cooking.

Do you have ways of cooking grains? Recipes you've committed to memory? Write here.

Like I said, I cook all loose things the same way. I'll talk about grains here (millet, sorghum, rice, wheatberries, whatever you have) but this would apply to beans or lentils, too.

1) Fill about a third of the pot with grains. Add water so the grains are submerged, and then some. Usually I have an inch or less of water on top.

2) Turn the heat to high, and allow the pot to near a boil or come to a boil. At that point, turn the heat down to medium low, stir it, then put a lid on it and let it cook.

3) As you go around the kitchen, peek at the top from time to time. If you notice the water's gotten low, add a little more (best if it's hot from the kettle).

4) When it's almost cooked, I'll taste a bit and maybe stir or close the lid again until it feels done. Most often, I won't taste at all.

Eventually, whatever you're cooking will be done.

The takeaway: I want you to feel comfortable cooking **ALL LOOSE THINGS** this way. We humans cooked grains and beans long before we had measuring cups or back of box instructions. When you think about it intuitively—think about what grains might want: sustained heat. Boiling is just too aggressive—the grains or beans CAN cook that way, and in a pitch I might do that, but they like it better at a simmer, for the sake of their skin and evenness of cooking.

 Orzo and couscous are pastas, so instead we cook them like pastas, with rapid boiling water for a much shorter period of time.

Do grains or beans show up in your family? Write down some of the memories or associations here. Most of our cultures include them.

We went over overboiling earlier in the week, and I want to come back to this. Because with this way of cooking loose things, sometimes, you're going to overcook them. Overcooking is not a mistake, **it's a new direction.**

MANTRA

i stay open and curious to how things show up in the world. there are an infinite number of ways to be. nothing in my kitchen ever goes wrong. it's all good.

Overcooked grains open up whole new paths. There are many wonderful purposes for overcooked grains and beans, so no big deal if that happens—it's a good thing. Sticky grains mean they can hold things together for us.

This leads us to our final concept of the day which is **BINDING**.

Let's say you have a pot of brown rice that's still hot. Some of the grains are intact, but many of them are still in wet, sticky globs—especially toward the bottom of the pot.

In this case, you might remove the top grains, and keep the bottom half to mold. Sticky rice like this, or any other grain that might have been a little overcooked, is perfect for getting looser things (like, say, caramelized onions, boiled beets or sautéed zucchini) into patty form.

Once you've scooped the sticky item (that bottom half of the pot of rice) into a bowl, decide what you'd like to add for flavor and texture. For texture, options include everything from a can of black beans or lentils to cooked vegetables. For flavor, you could add the last bits of pesto sitting in a container, or anything else that calls you. Be sure to add a hearty glug of olive oil, too.

If you're making **falafel**, you'll want to get some kind of mashed bean in there. As long as there are enough mashed beans (traditionally chickpea), they'll pass as a falafel.

Your goal is to **MAKE YOUR BATTER TASTE GOOD** so taste it every now and again as you add ingredients. Keep mixing and tasting.

Consider adding this mix to the food processor for a few pulses, especially if you want to break it down more and improve its hold. Adding an egg can also be good. Once you have your batter, mold into patties and place them in the pan to fry up.

Now go practice! Here's the challenge today. Cook some loose thing, grains, beans, whatever you want. DON'T use a recipe to cook it. If you overboil—make something moldable.

Tomorrow we'll cook again with pots, a different way. I'll see you then.

WEEK 2 / DAY SEVEN

Blanching, steaming and double boiling. Today, you'll learn about all three and practice one.

While we simplify systems of cooking—pot, pan, oven—I also want to make sure you get some of the less common terms and methods too, so you feel equipped and confident if they're mentioned or if you need them.

Let's start with blanching! First, what is it?

BLANCHING—is like jumping into an ice bath after hot tubbing. It wakes food up and stops the cooking process.

We think of foods as either raw (carrots in a bag) or cooked (carrots coming out of the oven) but blanching is somewhere in between the two.

Foods we can blanch are those that don't require a lot of cooking, that are happily edible in their raw state. Think about asparagus or broccoli, versus a beet or sweet potato.

82

How to blanch: To blanch asparagus or broccoli, you'd expose the vegetable to salty boiling water for a quick, intense period of time, maybe a minute or two minutes, then plunge it into cold water.

Why we'd do it: It keeps vegetables close to their raw state in terms of crunch and color, but lets them cook a little for more softness. Some people feel it accentuates the taste of vegetables.

To try it today: Go into your kitchen and choose a more delicate vegetable. Think of something that you'd be happy eating raw, but don't choose lettuce.

Now, bring a pot of water to a boil like we did earlier this week. (Add some salt to it.) Meanwhile, prepare a bowl of ice water.

Drop the vegetables in the boiling pot and allow to cook for a minute or two under large bubbles. Drain by throwing all the contents of the pot into a colander, and drop the vegetables in the ice water. After a bit, drain the contents again, and enjoy your blanched vegetable.

This is a way to make vegetables brighter on a crudité platter. ⌐ Platter of raw vegetables with dips you see at parties ⌐

Now, let's move on to two more methods.

Steaming and double boiling. Let's review what we know. Boiling is when you really need to get in there—with heat. Simmering is gentler. And then there's steaming and double boiling—two sort of fancy ways to use your pots.

Let's first talk about **steaming**.

If something is very delicate, like spinach, you can cook it with the STEAM of some boiling water instead of the boiling water itself.

How would you do this? Think, human! How about, let's place a colander on top of a pot and— then—cover it with a lid? YAAAAS. This is steaming.

Steam rises from the water and cooks the food. People steam with steamer baskets (foldable colanders) and also metal colanders, and they usually put only an inch or two of water in the pot if they use a steamer basket.

Up to you. The idea is to harness steam to cook.

Got it? Try it today if you'd like. But first, let's go over **double boiling.**

Double boiling is when you use a second pot instead of a colander. You place the second pot or metal bowl inside a larger pot, like resting on top of the water.

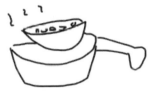

Melt some chocolate chips this way and you'd be double boiling them.

Today's exercise is to practice one of these three methods: blanching, steaming or double boiling. And remember—all of this is using heat to cook food. If you were to come up with a new method, the world could easily embrace that method, too. If you feel lost on how to do some aspect of the process, follow your instinct. You've got this! Go with your flow and I'll see you tomorrow.

WEEK THREE

WE'LL DO MORE COOKING THIS WEEK—AND PROGRESS A BIT MORE!

Again, we'll go slowly and take challenges one at a time, day by day. To recap last week, cooking is choosing which way to heat food.

Generally, the heartier a vegetable, the longer it will take to cook. A carrot will take longer to cook than a tomato and a potato will take longer to cook than broccoli—whether you use the oven, a pot, or a pan.

When you go into your kitchen and decide how you're going to cook something—pot, pan, or oven—you're cooking! You're making choices. YOUR choices. YOUR cooking.

There are the two primary styles of cooking: quick and strong, or low and slow. If you're searing a piece of meat, you may want to think quick and strong. If you're building a soup, you might think low and slow. Low heat. Slow going. Keep these ideas in mind as we move on through the challenges this week.

WEEK 3 / DAY ONE
Roasting and baking.

Last week we cooked with a pan and a pot. Now let's cook with the oven.

To start, if you're using the oven, you've decided to cook with hot air. This process will be slow, steady, and, in general, drying, unless you choose to immerse the food in liquid before you put it in.

Cooking food in the oven is great because it doesn't require much monitoring. Plus, it's out of your way so you can use yourself and your space to make other stuff.

When I was a private chef, I aimed to have one or two things in the oven at all times. I'd have a pan of broccoli and a deep dish of casserole, say, on two racks in the oven. When the broccoli finished, I'd get something else ready to put in there. Consider using your oven in this passive way.

Before we begin, go lie face-down on your floor.
Take a few deep breaths and stretch out long!

OK, back to our oven fun.

Q. WHAT TEMPERATURE IS GOOD FOR WHAT?
A. 400F WORKS FOR BASICALLY EVERYTHING.

People look to recipes to see what temperature
dishes take—but, truthfully, 400F works for
basically everything.

If you want to cook a bunch of stuff and aren't sure
what you want to cook yet, walk into the kitchen
and put the oven on 400F. Then, get chopping.

If you know you're only making baked goods, 350F
would be a more typical choice. If you're in a rush
and roasting vegetables, go with something higher
like 450F or 500F.

But remember, you're just trying to heat something up.

The hotter it is in there, the faster it will cook. The
cooler, the slower. You'll be tasting or looking for

status updates, and then, at some point, you'll take it out when you like it enough.

What if you use a really low temperature?
From time to time, you'll hear people talk about dehydrators—special little ovens that chefs (especially raw chefs) use to 'dehydrate' food, or cook food at lower temperatures. With dehydrators, you're 'cooking' food at lower temps like 130F.

At low temperatures with your oven, though, you can find the spirit of this effect. Try 275F to bake granola (oats, egg whites or not, whatever else you want, oil, and some sweetener, all tossed up.)

What's broiling? If you turn the oven dial to "broil," in a few minutes, a live, controlled fire (or a hot coil, depending) will appear on the top of the oven. This is good for singeing anything you put on that top rack.

If you have something that's already fully cooked, like a casserole full of pasta, you might sprinkle cheese on top and pop it in to broil for a minute. Whenever you want to toast bread but don't have a toaster, use the 'broil' feature to toast bread (be sure to keep a close eye after three or so minutes. The bread will brown quickly.)

Alright, ready for your challenge? It's simple. Cook something in your oven using one of its lower temperatures. That's it! What you cook in there is up to you. Have fun!

If you like what you made enough, include it below as your first recipe in this book. Enjoy your process

My Low Temp Recipe

and I'll see you tomorrow.

WEEK 3 / DAY TWO
Chop in your own way.

Chopping. Let's get into it.

First things first, establish a flat surface. When you're starting to cut something—from a sweet potato to a watermelon to a pineapple—make sure the food is sturdy. This means: get a flat surface down on the cutting board with your first cut. It's much safer than cutting into a wobbly object.

You can chop things however you'd like. There are no real rules, but keep in mind three things:

1) Evenness in size is going to make for consistent cooking. Experiment to find your favorite method for each vegetable and stick with it for a while. I most often cut onions one of two ways.

2) Keep it simple and don't overcomplicate. All chopped shapes will do just fine, and if you're roasting, many things left whole will eventually start to cook beautifully if you have the time.

3) Consider the shape of something before you cook it. There's a method of assembling chicken called spatchcocking, which you do by cutting out the chicken's backbone with a pair of heavy scissors and then flattening it out in a pan like a butterfly.

Because you're doubling the surface area, the bird will cook much faster. It's an extreme example of how shape matters when we chop and cook.

You can apply this principle to cooking all kinds of things. If you put a whole potato in, it's going to cook a lot slower than if you slice it in half or cut it into cubes. In general, the smaller the parts, the faster it will cook. Grated vegetable pieces are among the smallest, so those will cook very quickly. Hence why you can make hash browns quickly, but not many other kinds of potato dishes.

Today, as you cook (anything you want) focus your attention on your chopping. As you chop, think about turning objects face down so you're chopping into a sturdy object. Chop however you want. If you want, chop as lazy as you want. It will define the cooking in a certain way, and that's awesome.

WEEK 3 / DAY THREE
Explore cuisines.

Many people think of different cuisines when they think about cooking. There's a lot of truth in this—food does often fit into certain cultural territories—but before we start, I want to say this:

> THERE'S A LOT OF OVERLAP, AND THERE ARE MANY SUBCULTURES OF CUISINES WITHIN EVERY NATION. THROUGH OUR LIFETIMES—TRAVEL, FRIENDS, AND STUDY—WE'LL ALL LEARN MORE AND MORE. CHANCES ARE, YOU ALREADY HAVE QUITE A FEW CUISINES IN YOUR HEAD.

Let's explore your sense of cuisines, and cook from that place today. When I think of **Thai** and wanting to cook in a way that borrows from this culture, I think: **peanut butter, green onions, red pepper, garlic, cashews, shrimp, fish sauce**.

When you think **Italian**, you might think: **basil, pasta, tomatoes, garlic, onions, olives, cucumbers, green onions**.

When you think **Mexican,** you might think:
tortillas, lime, corn, beans, avocados.

Fill out as many cultures as you can think of,
naming as many tastes or ingredients as you
associate. Ask the people around you to join in. Try
to do a few subcultures (Louisiana, for instance.)

Debate as you go and look things up as needed.

Now, for today's challenge. It splits in two: choose one.

> **1) Cook within one of the cultures you wrote.** Collect the ingredients from your kitchen, and enjoy the exploration.

> **2) Cook in a way that blends two or three cultures.** I did so the other night when I—cooked leeks and tomatoes (Italian) with nutritional yeast in a 1960s casserole dish (Americana health culture), then added Korean kimchi and chopped leftover veggie pizza and cooked it until it was oozing and crusty. (It was delicious, served with a big handmade wooden spoon sitting out in the backyard with Christmas lights on, a night in very early fall.)

Choose your challenge, and go for it.

WEEK 3 / DAY FOUR
Learn something new.

Before we get cooking, let's start today with
a ritual. It's called **RAIN**—and it's one of my
favorites—which I learned from Tara Brach, the
meditation teacher. I do this in the middle of the
night if I wake up with a challenging emotion, and
because it lands us in the realm of nurturing, it's
relevant to cooking. The letters of **RAIN** stand for:
Reflect, Allow, Investigate and Nurture.

Reflect—how are you feeling? Can you name it?
Notice.

Allow—say to yourself, 'this belongs,' this feeling
belongs, make space. This one is often my key.
Wow—ok, no problem here. This is part of the
human experience.

Investigate—where does this feeling show up in
your body? Chest? Head? When you find where the
emotion shows up in your body, place your
hand there.

Nurture—what does a being who feels this way need most? A certain word, phrase, or idea? A bath? A type of food? A decision?

Cooking is emotional. It finds you in all kinds of states. Whenever you need support, as my friend Julana and I say to each other, "do RAIN."

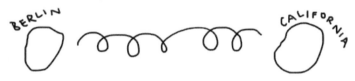

Today, write your RAIN down here.

R

A

I

N

Now, you're ready for some cooking. Today, our challenge is to make the time to honor something you said you wanted to learn.

That's right! Let's go back to that list you wrote on page 8. Scan what you have in your kitchen, then pick one of the three.

One where you feel you have enough of the core ingredients to proceed (like if you chose pasta, do you have flour? If you want to 'make better salmon', do you have salmon?) and write it here:

Today, I'm going to explore and learn:

_____

Now, set a ten minute alarm and browse the Internet. Search, click, read. ~~Screen shot, screen shot, screen shot.~~

Pick up ideas about the process and supporting ingredients. You'll find LOTS of ideas! Let your mind pick up what you like—and give you ideas of what you have in your kitchen.

Then, put the phone down, and head to your kitchen to cook. No recipes. Go from what you've learned, and let yourself improvise.

Be free if you want! Or, if it's nurturing to your vibe today, write your steps and quantities down while you're going.

Be specific or vaaaague

2 Tbs	a handful
¼ cup	a big glug

I'll leave room for you here to write it…

_____ 'S RECIPE FOR _____

-

-

-

-

-

-

When you're done—eating and cleaning up—write about it: How did it go today? What did you learn about the topic you chose?

I'll see you tomorrow. We're doing more cooking! A different challenge, a different way.

WEEK 3 / DAY FIVE
Make a drink.

Today's let's talk about DRINKS, something we do even more than eating. What do you drink most often? _____

Write your day out in beverages, morning to night:

Wake-10am

10am-2pm

2pm-5pm

5pm-Sleep

I start my day with something bright. I think about when my stomach is empty as the time when it absorbs the most. Think of all the surface area (no food yet.) First thing, I'll drink lemon juice, boiled ginger and turmeric, hemp seed oil and raw honey. Or even just green tea. THEN, I'll drink coffee, eat, and so on.

YOUR FIRST THING DRINK

Old one: **New one:**

What would you say is your FAVORITE drink? Write any down that come to mind.

Today's challenge is to make a special drink for yourself—recipe free.

Look in your fridge and cocktail cabinet and gather what you'd like. I love to gather sparkling water, juices, tinctures (mushrooms, St. John's Wort), bitters, and garnishes. I love big ice cubes too.

The only rule today is that your drink needs to contain more than one ingredient AND a garnish.

103

A GARNISH—It can be ANYTHING—a lemon, some mint, a dash of cinnamon, the stranger the better. Today, write your recipe down as you go. Use this as a structure.

MY _____ DRINK

A lot of _____

A little _____

And _____

And _____

And _____

How does it taste? Write it down.

If you could put this drink on a menu, what would you call it?

Good job today! See you tomorrow.

104

WEEK 3 / DAY SIX
Create your own cleaning spray.

You're doing more cooking now, which means you're doing more cleaning up too! To support that part of your cooking life, let's **make a DIY cleaner**.

Right up there with labeling your food, DIY cleaners give you a fresh and fancy feeling with minimal expense. Let's put the time in, and get you upgraded in this way.

Your Own All Purpose Cleaning Spray. First, shake off any expectations! Have fun—this will be YOURS. Now, search your house and find a spray bottle.

It could be an almost empty, branded one (that's how I started making mine), or it could be a new, empty one (the amber colored or clear ones). If you don't have a spray bottle, find another kind of bottle. Whatever you've got is great.

Next, search your house for any of these you can find: white vinegar, hydrogen peroxide, and baking soda. (Great! What did you find? Write it here.)

(
This will be the basis of your cleaning solution. If you have two of them, awesome.
)

Now, empty your bottle and fill it partway with the ingredient you found. White vinegar, hydrogen peroxide, or a solid shake of baking soda. Don't be too serious about the portions, and don't bother looking anything up (on the Internet, you'll find SUCH a range of what people do)!

Follow your instinct…cleaning up and the instinct to clean are within you—use your nose and eyes.

Next, fill the bottle nearly to the top with water, or if you have it, distilled water (even better, because it will last even longer). People say normal water will last 2 weeks (or, if you want to be extra safe, keep it in the fridge. I don't! I just keep it on my counter.)

Now, let's add some fancy stuff. Run around the house and see if you have any of the following: lemons or any essential oils (especially lavender, peppermint, lemon, orange, tea tree, grapefruit, or eucalyptus), any fresh stiff herbs like rosemary or thyme.

If you have lemons, squeeze a whole one in, avoiding seeds. Such a cool cleaning agent! For essential oils, do some drops. You know what you like! Anywhere from 3 drops to 20 drops is alright. Close top and shake! If you have a dried herb, drop it in the bottle.

Now, spray on a surface and sniff. Like it? Wipe it up with a paper towel. Record your recipe in this book and use it to clean up your kitchen as you continue to progress as a cook.

If you have labels—add one to the bottle. "ALL PURPOSE SPRAY" or "MAGIC" or "GOOD VIBES." (If you smell something that makes you think of a word or phrase, use that word or phrase!) Tape and sharpie also great.

_____ 'S ALL-PURPOSE CLEANER

AKA _____

This spray will be an essential part of your cooking routine. At the end of most nights, I use my DIY spray and paper towel to wipe up all counters and leave the kitchen smelling clean for the morning.

Go do that now and I'll see you tomorrow!

WEEK 3 / DAY SEVEN
Write a menu.

Today I want you to practice writing a menu. You can be practical about it, or poetic. There's no wrong method. To write your menu today—

Think of the season and current weather, the ingredients you have in your house, and who will be eating the meal. Below are sample menu items to inspire you, followed by blank phrases for you to fill. Look through your kitchen and fill in based on what you find.

Cauliflower macadamia soup with crispy sage leaves
_____ _____ *soup with* _____ _____
_____

Duck confit, roasted squash, and cranberry compote with cinnamon & orange
_____ _____, *roasted* _____, *and*
_____ _____ *with* _____ & _____

Slivered kale, Brussels & toasted almond salad in a tart lemon pecorino dressing
_____ _____, _____ & _____
_____ _____ *in a* _____ _____ *dressing*

109

Buttermilk chicken w/ roasted pink radishes &
preserved lemons
_____ *chicken w/ roasted* _____
_____ *& preserved* _____

Sliced persimmons, berries & dark chocolate in
bowls to share
Sliced _____, _____ **&** _____
in bowls to share

Slow cooked squid with olives and parsley
Slow cooked _____ **with** _____
and _____

Lobster salad with butter asparagus
_____ *salad with* _____ _____

Avocados filled with Old Bay shrimp salad
_____ *filled with* _____

Baskets of corn bread
Baskets of _____ _____

You can include whatever you want on your menu.
Doesn't have to be just food.

When I had my popup restaurant in San Francisco,
my menus were less tactical and more creative
because I was my own client and the people who
followed relied on the whimsy of it.

During this time, I was teaching yoga and living on the beach, so a lot of the references in those menus came from those aspects of my life. On one menu, I had people choose their music and gave them headsets. On another, I offered add-ons like shots of algae or a take-away hand cream.

Now that you've warmed yourself up, write a menu, drafting it in the blank space here.

You can hand-write it, or type it up and print it, but I want you to be able to hold it in your hands. Start by going into your fridge and pantry to decide on your main course. How many courses do you want? How about sides, and dessert?

If you're stuck, the menu could be really simple like 'Milk, peanut butter and jelly, carrot sticks" and then see what actions or language you'd want to add to that. The point is, I want you to use your words. Connect language to food.

Good job this week! I'll see you tomorrow for the start of week four.

MENU

WEEK FOUR

IT'S WEEK FOUR. WE'VE COOKED A BUNCH.

We've talked. We've reflected some too. This week, we're going to work on your cooking identity as well as dive into some of the more experimental and challenging aspects of cooking without recipes. The first half of the week will be reflection exercises. The second, cooking.

Ready to go?

WEEK 4 / DAY ONE
Record your trusted recipes.

Before we move away from recipes, let's celebrate them:

Recipes are great! They're great for making the <u>best</u> crème brûlée <u>EVER</u>

For scrolling around the Internet for the most amazing croissant in the world. For passing dishes down through your family.

I like them for replicating a very specific dish or cocktail from a specific restaurant, and I like them on behalf of any chef who LOVES them.

Any other reasons you love recipes? What are your go-to sources for recipes—blogs, newsletters, books, friends or family members? Write your sources down here.

Now, I don't want to bash recipes. But I also want to start a wave of interest in questioning them.

What's wrong with recipes? For everyday cooking, they slow us down and distance us from our senses. Comfort in managing ingredients is replaced by comfort in reading recipes (I can totally make coffee cake—just let me find that recipe I love first!) Missing ingredients feel like a dead end. Grocery shopping gets expensive, and often ends up wasteful too (ever bought that big thing of dill because a recipe said you need a teaspoon of it?)

When I stopped using recipes, I felt the identity of becoming a good cook first with myself (competence, ease, joy, my own little idiosyncratic tricks and habits) and later with others, when I started extending this life I'd found professionally.

In my opinion, we're all equipped to cook without recipes. And I wouldn't have become a professional chef unless I'd quit them.

Best of all—returning to yourself, your own creative flow and judgments, leads to something MAGICAL. To me, it connected me to that glowing identity of really knowing how to cook. The confidence that I can cook for a lifetime—no matter who's around and what's in the kitchen at hand. YES—EVEN— for baked goods. Especially for baked goods! It's a simple but revolutionary act. Departing from prescribed rules and boundaries, returning to what is fundamentally HUMAN and INSIDE of us.

Yep, all those rules are inside you.

Now, chances are you have a few recipes you love. I do too! I want you to go get those and write them down, in your own handwriting. Give the items names, "Brownies," or "Super Gooey Brownies" or "Annie's brownies" or however you think of them.

Share the ones you love most with your community.

Recipe

PREP TIME	RECIPE FOR	COOK TIME
_____	_____	_____

INGREDIENTS	DIRECTIONS

Recipe

PREP TIME	**RECIPE FOR**	COOK TIME

INGREDIENTS   **DIRECTIONS**

INGREDIENTS	DIRECTIONS

Recipe

PREP TIME	**RECIPE FOR**	COOK TIME

INGREDIENTS   **DIRECTIONS**

INGREDIENTS	DIRECTIONS

Recipe

PREP TIME	RECIPE FOR	COOK TIME
_____	_____	_____

INGREDIENTS	DIRECTIONS

Recipe

WEEK 4 / DAY TWO
Acknowledge what you know.

Yesterday, we gave credit to recipes you've inherited or found from others. Today, let's talk about YOU and your cooking.

When you think of ONE THING you cook that turns out great, what is it? (Think of everything you make—from breakfast to sandwiches to dinner, drinks and dessert.)

Write it proudly here.

_____

Is it a recipe, a habit, a method, a step, a thought, a full dish? _____

And where did you learn it? From someone who taught you? From experimentation on your own?

_____

With building blocks like these, we grow as cooks. We learn from what gets passed down, and we learn from what we create ourselves. We get closer to that feeling of being good at cooking. We grow in CONFIDENCE.

Alright, you're on a roll—what do you like to do with EGGS? Any special way you do them? (I'll go left, you go right.)

Put a pan over medium heat. Put a chunk of butter down in a pan, Once melted, place a deli slice of cheese down in the pan. Once it's cooking, crack an egg on top, carefully holding the egg in place on top of the cheese with the shell. Release when you can do so without it sliding off. Once cooked to your liking, sprinkle parmesan on top. Serve on a toasted bagel or croissant.

In the kitchen, confidence comes from making mistakes and doing things your own way. Mostly, it's the inner knowing that you can figure anything out. That you know what to do—or you'll figure it out.

Competence in the kitchen requires a spirit of confidence—a moving forward, a spirit of let's do it. That's why I want to spend today on confidence.

This is a phrase I like in tapping, an emotional freedom technique. In the practice, you tap on various parts of your body (chin, top of the head, collar bones) and say phrases out loud. Often, you're repeating after a practitioner, but you can do it yourself.

Let's try it now. With four fingers tapping either side of your hairline, say the phrase out loud, slowly and deliberately. "I know what to do."

It's comforting. It's always true. It's the crux of how I became a chef and it's how I know you can too. Other phrases I like from tapping are "All is well" and "I let go of being general manager of the universe." You can tap anywhere on your body that you want.

Tomorrow, as you bake without recipes (maybe for the first time), you may become uncomfortable. If that happens, you have a new tool. I want you to say to yourself, "I know what to do."

"I know what to do."

How would you finish the following sentences?

Have no _____.

Move forward even when _____.

Give food to _____.

WEEK 4 / DAY THREE
Prepare to change.

Today begins my favorite period in our whole journey together. It's the day you start your journey baking without recipes. Now, I hear a lot of things when I talk to people about this.

I hear, "I feel like I can cook without recipes when it comes to savory food, but with baked goods, I'm just not familiar enough with the portions."

And it's a great argument. I'm almost convinced when I hear someone say that.

Or I hear, "Baking is so scientific and precise. You can't just wing baking. It's not that kind of thing."

And again, not bad thinking. I totally get it.

Here's the thing about baking without recipes. It's a little bit of a trade-off, I suppose, and that's me being generous to the side that uses recipes. (Because a lot of baked goods still don't turn out too well, even with recipes.)

When you bake without recipes—a lot, all the time—the pros are very clear. You can go into your kitchen and make a batch of cookies, a batch of scones, banana bread, brownies, whatever you want—in literally a matter of minutes.

The downside is—sometimes you get salty cookies. Now, most often I'll make even a salty cookie situation great (by wedging them with sweet jam and powdering them with powdered sugar, for instance).

And in reality, these bad baked goodies are maybe one in fifty. Maybe one in twenty. You'll figure out your own situation. The thing is—when you bake without recipes—and something comes out good, really good, juicy, awesome—it's yours to be proud of. Really yours.

And honestly, it happens a lot. You never get the same thing twice (makes the projects so exciting) and you can pull up to any ski house at 8pm—flash around the kitchen with whatever flours and sugars were there—and make people a plate of goodness by the time everyone's taken showers. It's fun!

If baking without recipes sounds totally alien and scary, here's how I go about it. This will make it easier for you, and we'll go into this topic to learn and practice several times together until you feel comfortable.

So, first off, I get my idea for what I want to bake by looking around my kitchen. Let's do that in yours right now. Go look around and notice what you have.

Notice what you have in terms of **flours** (this would include all the typical and non-typical flours as well as something like oats which you could quickly blend into a flour in your blender.)

Notice what you have in terms of **fats** (this would include all butters and oils, and also things like peanut butter, almond butter or coconut cream.)

Notice what you have in terms of **sweeteners** (sugars of all kinds, honeys, syrups—but also even hot cocoa powder or dates or bananas is worth noticing for this category. I think of extracts in this category too—vanilla extracts or almond extract or whatever you're lucky enough to have on hand).

Just notice, browse and see—let your mind light up with ideas. Get excited about what you could create.

Do you have **eggs**? If not, flax seeds or flax meal? If you have flax seeds, you'll grind them in a coffee grinder to make them meal, then combine with a little water (about twice the amount as you have meal) and that can act like your egg (they call it a flax egg). You can also grind chia seeds and—if you have none of these—you can still bake without them.

Notice what you have in terms of **baking soda or baking powder**. If you have baking soda, you'll add a dash to your flours (dry stuff) and if you have baking powder, you'll add a little more than a dash (still a dash, but think a little heavier.)

Notice what you have in terms of **fillings**. Look for chocolate chips, oats, dried cranberries, nuts, and anything else creative you have like M&Ms.

Tomorrow, we'll bake something using what you've discovered! Keep envisioning what you might want to create and tomorrow we'll go at it.

WEEK 4 / DAY FOUR
Bake without recipes.

Today might feel like the most challenging of all our days together. You're going to bake without using any recipes or reference points. More than that—you'll do so without us going over the topic together (that's tomorrow.)

Why? Because I want you to light up that part of you that knows how to bake from the first chance. So many little lessons come right UP to us when we're in the process ourselves.

So, right, for some of you—this might be a new, first-time experience! And NEW experiences are great. That's how we learn. If this makes you nervous, stick with it and deepen your breath or pause for a hot drink if that nervousness shows up in the process.

The flow will invite you back in. Keep it simple.

Follow this simple five-step process below and you will have accomplished today's goal. If you get stuck on a number, do a **WOOP** (wish, outcome, obstacle, plan) on the side of the page. First question is a reflection! Spend a little time on it.

1. What did you notice yesterday that you want to bake with today?

2. Now, for ACTION. Pull all the related ingredients out and get yourself a big bowl or two, some spoons and an environment (music, lighting) that you like.

3. Then, without looking at ANYTHING, get baking. Put together a baked good. Don't expect ANYTHING. Expect nothing except your ability to finish this challenge. Go through your own process, letting yourself question things and then make decisions.

4. When your item is in the oven, write about your process below, exactly how it was.

WHAT DID YOU LEARN?

WHAT ASPECTS OF YOUR PROCESS WOULD YOU REPEAT FOR SURE? (Write the things that went well even if they feel obvious—e.g. not burning my hand in the oven, using the right amount of milk, anything, anything.)

5. Taste what you made and write down

  A. HOW DOES IT TASTE?

  B. HOW DOES IT LOOK?

  C. WHAT'S ITS NAME?

  D. WOULD YOU MAKE IT AGAIN?

I'll see you tomorrow! You're doing SO great. WOW.

WEEK 4 / DAY FIVE
Let's bake together.

Today, we'll get back in the kitchen for more baking. I'll teach you how I go about baking without recipes, and you write notes as you have your own insights. Okay, let's begin. One way to think about baking is—

Baked Goods = Wet stuff + Dry stuff + Fillings

In baking texts, you'll often see people mixing wet stuff in one bowl, then dry stuff in another, but I don't do that and I don't find it to be necessary for everyday baking.

I use one bowl to make everything.

Occasionally, I even use the vessel I'm going to bake in (Pyrex dishes are great for this) to mix everything up. Baked goods equal wet stuff plus dry stuff plus fillings? Yes, let's break each part down more.

1. Make your wet stuff. Start with a fat. What do you have in the kitchen? Butter? Coconut oil? Only olive oil? Only vegetable oil? There are loads of fats and all of them are going to bake us something good. Choose one, and drop a big chunk or glug it on in. Don't worry too much about the quantity. For now, air on the side of extra.

Once I have that in the bowl, I'll mix in a sweetener. So many options—could be brown or white sugar, honey, agave nectar, whatever you have. If I'm making brownies, sometimes this step will be Swiss Mix hot chocolate mix.

For the sweetener, I pour whatever amount in I feel like that day: often I'm being healthy and airing on the side of low sugar, but sometimes I just want a classic chocolate chip cookie taste or I have fewer other sweet ingredients than normal and I go heavier.

For instance, if I was making sugar cookies or shortbread, I'd add more sugar than if I know I'm about to make chocolate chip cookies.

Next, if I have eggs, I'll crack two eggs into my bowl. If I only have one, I'll do one. If it's a bigger crowd, three. Don't let me confuse you though—get in the habit of cracking two eggs.

Mix those up with a fork or spoon. Now, if you don't have eggs, do the flax trick we went over yesterday (flaxmeal + eyeballing about twice as much water), or use chia seeds. If you don't have any of this, just skip! It's okay. You can still bake. (In fact, I did so just now—chocolate chip banana cookies, so great.)

Lastly, if you have vanilla extract around or any other wet stuff that's inspiring you, add some.

That's your wet stuff! (if you're doing cookies)

If you're making cake or muffins, I'd add milk at this point. A big glug, not to worry now about how much. If you have yogurt, add a scoop of that for extra creaminess and a little tang.

TO REVIEW, OUR WET STUFF IS:
FAT, SUGAR, EGGS, EXTRACTS, AND
MAYBE A MILK LIQUID.

2. Now, let's make the dry stuff.

Off to one side of your wet bowl (or in a separate bowl, if you want) add a heavy toss of flour or something flour-like such as almond flour,

Almond flour is just almonds that have been pulsed down into tiny little pieces. Same thing for oat flour or rice flour. So if all you have is the whole element—oats, almonds, even if you have walnuts, say—you can make any of these fancier flours just by using the pulse function on your food processor or even your coffee grinder.

Once you have your flour, add a little salt and a dash of baking soda, or a dash of baking powder (people say three times as much if you're using baking powder, but they both work.) Don't measure. Don't stress. Less is more. If you put too much, you'll taste it—just do a little for now.

Mix that little pile around with a fork, avoiding the wet stuff underneath as best you can. No big deal. Now you've got your dry stuff!

Once that part is combined, slowly mix it together with the wet stuff. Check in with yourself—how does that batter feel? Is it pourable? Or sticky? You can add more milk at this point…or more flour.

3. Now let's do the fillings.

This is where the character of the project comes to fruition. I'm a big fan of throwing a lot of variety in—it gives you a loving, hearty, and unique finished baked good. Nuts, seeds, oats, and chopped dried fruit add fiber and also mitigate texture problems. Chopped bananas are a blessing to anything.

> **HOW THIS STAGE FEELS AND LOOKS:** At this point in the process, all of my cabinets are open and I'm scanning with my eyes to determine what fits my intention.

When looking for fillings, consider perishables that feel compatible with the project. Is there an abundance of overripe nectarines on your counter? Chop those up. If I have a lot of low-quality granola, or granola-based cereal for some reason, I might consider throwing it in at this point, too.

Taste the batter if you're up for it!

Some people don't like to taste batter if it has raw eggs in it. I don't mind, and enough of the baked goods I make don't have eggs in them to even out my risks. It's up to you. If you're a kid, ask your parents and discuss.

Tasting the batter helps you to detect if you forgot something (like salt, which is helpful for making your taste buds notice the sweetness.) In my experience—if the batter tastes good, your finished product probably will too.

If you taste anything a little funky (too sweet, not sweet enough, too much baking powder), you'll adjust from there until you love the batter and know its time has come to head to the oven. If you don't taste batters, that's even more fun in a way—a great mystery what's ahead. You can gauge a lot through texture too. We'll go over that more in depth tomorrow.

Next, send that baby to the oven.

First, butter, oil or spray the inside of whatever tin

you're using (I like to keep the butter wrappers when I finish sticks in a dish next to my oven for this purpose exactly). Once you've heated the oven to 350F, slide it in. Take a look after about 10 minutes, then maybe 15 minutes, and just see how it's going.

The less liquidy the batter, the sooner you'll want to check it out. So maybe look at cookies a little past 9 minutes or so. Just keep an eye on them— and a nose.

Most things smell good when they're ready or moments from being ready. If you want, poke them with your finger, or slit a knife into the center if it's a deep cake or bread. You know that trick already, right? If the knife comes out with wet batter on it, it needs more time. But also, the thing is going to keep baking a little when it comes out and you can always put it back in for a little bit. Plus, the gooier the better, in many cases.

Today, I want you to practice making a baked good without a recipe. It could be anything you want. Either follow along with my process or just try on your own. However your baked good tastes today, you're making great progress.

Draw pictures of the result when it gets out, and remember—name it once you've tasted it—not before!

WEEK 4 / DAY SIX
Explore batters.

How did yesterday go? Did you like what you made? Whether you did or you didn't, you're on track. You've started to turn those parts of yourself on that know how to choose volumes, combine things, and create baked goods—from your own instinct.

Your baking will continue to get better and better.

As an exercise today, let's think about your batter from yesterday. Start by describing it. How did it feel, look, and move:

While we don't need recipes to bake, we do need a sense of what batter should feel like for different projects. Batters are distinct and belong on a range:

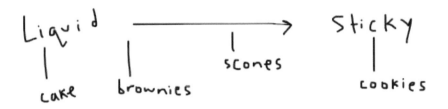

One essential aspect of baking well regards getting that batter to a state in which you want it—getting familiar with what cookie batter feels like versus cake batter. You can make adjustments all the way up until the item goes in the oven.

While cookies don't generally have milk in their batters, even if you have added milk—you can always course correct and have cookies at the end of your session.

Today, let's think about the batters of your favorite things. You've baked a lot in your life (I know)—and you remember how things feel. Draw on the left, describe the batter on the right.

No baking today! Tomorrow, we'll look at a specific ingredient which is an angelic addition to most baked goods. See you then!

144

WEEK 4 / DAY SEVEN
Bake from what you see.

Baking without recipes stumps a lot of people, so that's why we're spending some time on it. Today I'm going to walk you through one example of a baked good I made without a recipe: why I made it, what the process looked like, and how it turned out. At the end, you'll bake yourself!

It's not some kind of PERFECT STORY

Starring in my story is a banana. A banana is always a good idea, especially if it's overripe. If you choose to use bananas in your baked goods, you'll most often either mush it into the wet stuff at the beginning with the back of a fork, or chop it up and treat it like individual fruit chunks as a filling.

See? Wet stuff, dry stuff, and fillings. So much inside of that is up to you! Alright, on to the story.

Blackberry bread: it's midday on an afternoon and I'm eating the gooiest, most delicious blackberry bread, coincidentally living at that farmhouse I told you about in France...

It started because I noticed that my last banana, the banana sitting on my counter, was speckled with brown dots.

I also knew that I had a couple eggs (from the chickens, who, by the way had not been putting out too many of those lately.) I knew I had wheat flour and both cow and soy milk.

With that knowledge, I turned on the oven. (Try to turn on the oven once you have your version of enough information. That will encourage you to create swiftly and cut out waiting time. Many times, turning on the oven gets me thinking, so I'll do it with not much information at all as to what I'll cook.)

For all baked goods, like I've told you, I use one bowl. So the bowl I usually take out is a good-enough sized bowl to not get my kitchen all fluffy with flour. In this situation, though, I didn't want to eat too much of this thing, so I chose a sort of medium one rather than my largest one.

I cracked two eggs on top of the mashed banana sort of to the side and fork-whisked the eggs right on top of the banana. Then I combined the banana mash and eggs, just with the fork.

At that point I went into my fridge and took out a Tupperware of sliced pears that I had prepped earlier in the morning. The pears were already starting to brown so I knew this was the right choice versus the apples I had cut, which I felt would cook more slowly because of their firmness and less sugar content. These pears are very sweet, and they come from a tree that throws them off and into the grass almost too quickly for me to save them. At that point, I threw them into the mash and smashed them in.

WET STUFF, THEN DRY STUFF.

From there I threw in some wheat flour. Guys, please don't stress about the amount of flour you throw in. Just think, what am I trying to make? I'm trying to make an oozy pudding kind of thing, more soft and wet than dry, hard, and doughy, so I'm not going to put so much in. I'm just using the flour here to sort of help hold it together and give it structure.

Next, I started stirring, preferring big, scooping, slow stirs rather than fast, little ones. This is because I know over-stirring will make things that have flour in them tougher, and I'm not trying to bite into something too tough today.

'Ooh. Do I want some butter in this thing?' I think.

Yesss, obviously. At this point, I realized I wanted to use some of the butter I have which would have been ideal to mix by hand with the flour or melt in a pot and mix into the first mushy liquid group. (Note: If I had melted it in a pot, I'd want to let it cool in any number of ways so it wouldn't cook the eggs.)

But, alas, no problem. Butter would participate a different way. I cut a slab of it with a butter knife and cut it up a few times to scatter the pieces of butter around. I may have made an attempt to mash the butter in a bit, then I buttered the base and sides of the casserole.

Ooh. Those blackberries! I see them in all their glory.

'Do they want to participate in this situation,' I think? Yesss, obviously. I pull the blackberries from the fridge. Most days out here I pick a big colander full of them and bring them home for a wash, dry and a Tupperware because I've noticed they last much longer in the fridge, probably because I'm not allowing fox mouth germs to prosper. (It's a thing out here! So much so that you're not supposed to pick blackberries below your hip.)

Anyway, I threw in the blackberries, mixed, and scooped the whole oozy thing into the casserole.

I didn't wonder whether it would be good. It would be good. There was no way for it not to be good.

I did wonder, in what way it would be good, and if I were in a professional context, I'd maybe wonder what exactly I'd end up naming it, and all of this is only fun and not stressful. I simply got in bed with a book, and checked it after 15 minutes or so, kept an eye, and took it out when I knew it was ready.

and it was delicious

Today, I want you to follow your own intuitive path with a baked good. Like my example in the kitchen in France, what's IN your kitchen is participating and giving you ideas. The food is like a co-collaborator.

Go for it. Walk through your kitchen and allow something to catch your eye. At that point, turn on the oven and go from there—start building. Use your senses and your intuition. Don't sweat proportions. Just throw in amounts that you think make sense. Worse case—you learn! You've got this!

WEEK FIVE

YOU'RE REALLY COOKING NOW!

I'm going to start treating you more like a cook this week, so I want you to start writing in the margins with your own preferences as often as you can. In other words, talk back!

If you haven't yet completed week four, I'm encouraging you to go back to it before moving on to this week. Some of these messages will make a lot more sense once you've started the experiential aspect of baking without recipes.

Thank you so much, and let's get started!

WEEK 5 / DAY ONE
Coming alive with cooking.

In my experience, becoming a good cook is the process of coming alive. It's a set of feelings.

What is alive? Alive is creative, joyful, fun, light-hearted, playful, bold, unworried, in the moment and curious. When you feel these emotions—in the kitchen—you are becoming a good cook. Think about how cooking felt last week for you. Did you feel a sense of flow or ease, even just momentarily? Write some of your feelings down here.

YOU'RE DOING GREAT.

As we continue cooking without recipes—you'll fumble a bit. It's natural and what we want! What I want you to keep in mind is: COMING ALIVE IS MESSY.

And after a while, most things, like 95% of things, are going to turn out awesome. You'll get intuitive, adaptable, agile—all these rewards of practicing.

Here are some of the principles to help you make the transition into cooking well without recipes. Read through them and write notes or draw along the margins as you go.

NOT RULES

1. Name things once they're done, not before.

You can have an idea of what something is going to be, but don't give it a name until it comes out of the oven—until you've seen, touched and tasted it. I like to let baked goods sit for about five minutes before tasting. It lets them settle into themselves.

Like we said when we discussed names, it's great to be given delicious chocolate cake, but NOT great if someone's calling it a brownie.

WAIT! THIS ISN'T A BROWNIE!!

To name something, don't just rely on the word attached to what you PLANNED to make. Go based on what's showing up to your **EYES**—how does it look? How is its shape? And to your **MOUTH**—what does it taste and feel like? Allow your **BRAIN** to give you the words and BAM—you've called the thing the right name.

If you're dealing with a baked good, once you let it cool off, add a post-it to the container where you'll store it—this will make your kitchen feel well cared for every time you walk in.

2. Nothing is a big deal.

Everything is fine—fixable and in progress. Other people around you will see ALL the things as a big deal—what?! The falafel's browning—what?! We're out of sour cream!—what?! The guests are coming in an hour—what?!

Part of your path as a good cook—the kitchen leader, essentially—is that nothing fazes you, nothing disturbs you, everything has a solution, and everything is more or less meant to be.

Are there aspects of leadership you want to note here, too? Maybe leadership in the kitchen means setting boundaries for little kids wanting endless cookies? Or maybe it means hosting on behalf of your household when people enter your home?

3. Believe in yourself.

Overcoming fear in the moment—in the kitchen—is like your jet pack. There were plenty of moments when I was cooking that my inner confidence came to rescue me from some looming fear.

I'd stand there in front of the crowded counter—groceries everywhere, and a flash of doubt would come over me: How do I know what to do with these dozen eggs? Why should I know what to do with them?

And then I'd give myself a gentle tap forward: I'm fine. I know what I'm doing. And I did. We all do. Cooking is not for the rare few. It's in all of us. Believe in yourself. This confidence is essential when it comes to becoming a great cook for all of us.

4. Be bold.

Most people who say they can't cook are just holding back. Give yourself permission to use extra—to be extra! Hurl it in. Go for it—especially when you're dealing with tasty items like chocolate chips or lemon or olive oil or walnuts.

Toss in a heap of cinnamon and see what happens. Use the whole bag of cornflakes. Throw the rest of your soda into the chili you're making. Find a way to use your candy corn from Halloween. Boldness builds character. It will make you **YOU** in the kitchen.

What are your tasty items? Some of the ingredients that feel kindred to you as a person?

5. Be resourceful.

If you've just finished a jar of jam, pour in some milk and shake it up to make strawberry milk. This goes for all bottles of wet stuff.

If it's tomato sauce or canned tomatoes, add some water, put the lid back on the container, shake it up, and throw it into any number of things that you're cooking (a soup, a sauce, whatever).

When you boil beets, you can use that beautiful pink water to substantiate something else, like enhancing the color and richness of a minestrone—or make it richer.

If you have extra broth hanging around, anything you'd cook using water, you'd be wise to cook it in that broth. Broth is beauty. And broth comes out of many cooking processes, not just from cooking meat.

I think of broth as all sorts of things. That briny water that mozzarella balls sit in? Or the sundried tomato oil or water that olives come in? Broth. Don't overthink it! Use what's tasty.

6. Prepare for your future self.

One thing that feels like good cooking to me is saving relishes, sauces, and things that come from take-out or your own cooking in small containers.

They're often so dense in taste and even nutritious stuff you wouldn't make yourself (fermented jicama?)—one restaurant's trade secret sauce or even just finely chopped onions.

Now, soy sauce packets and ketchups may be already too abundant—but keep an eye on the take out food rather than tossing the bag in the trash. See what you can save. There's gold in there.

Be a guardian of your fridge and fill it with things to encourage spontaneous joy. It's a great feeling to come home late at night with a group of friends who are hungry and realize you have spicy sweet pepper marmalade for nachos.

7. Give yourself time.

I have burnt a ton of nuts—and also coconut shavings—not giving them the time they need. I'll pump the heat on the pan to medium high— not daring to go fully high—and then I'll act like I've given those slivered almonds a good home and walk away to tend the oven. Doesn't work! They burn, they lose their subtlety, it's okay but unfortunate (I still use my poorly cared for nuts, anyway.) The learning is: give things time.

Finish this list with a few other cooking principles that come to mind for you.

8.

9.

10.

WEEK 5 / DAY TWO
Thicken a dish.

Today let's get back in the kitchen to cook. The lesson: thickening. It's a principle that will come into your cooking ALL the time.

So what does it mean to thicken something, and how do you do it?

Ingredients such as flour, cornstarch, ground oats and mashed beans help thicken a dish. So, let's say you're making a cherry pie. You might use cornstarch to thicken up the cherry filling, or jam.

When you add flour to a liquid in a pan, you are making a "rue." Doing so thickens what is otherwise a thin liquid into something creamy.

Béchamel sauce starts with onions and some butter. You slowly

SIDE NOTE You can also add cornstarch to shredded potatoes that you're about to mound up and fry, which also helps keep the color intact and adds to the crispiness (by drying out some of the wetness).

add flour, and then you slowly add milk, and any seasonings.

Hollandaise is another creamy sauce which you make by whisking egg yolk and lemon juice together, then applying gentle heat from below and drizzling in butter. Both were made because some human was trying to make a liquid delicious—and thicken it up!

THERE ARE ALL KINDS OF WAYS TO THICKEN SOMETHING, AND YOUR CHALLENGE TODAY IS TO PLAY WITH THIS IDEA OF THICKENING IN YOUR KITCHEN.

How about thinning? Sometimes, your project will be too thick so you'll want to thin it out. Thinning often means adding a liquid, like broth or water or milk. If you want a frittata to come out lighter, rather than thicker, add more milk to the batter when you're making it.

Or, let's say you want a fluffy cake batter rather than a heavier one—add some whipped egg whites to lighten it up.

Today—in your practice with thickening, start with a broth, and work ingredients into it from there. Use milks, fats, and any other ingredients in mind to progressively thicken the dish.

Tomorrow, we'll do a reflection exercise.

WEEK 5 / DAY THREE
Explore early food memories.

Now that you're cooking more often—people are going to ask you about food and cooking more. It's a reflection of your identity as a chef growing more central to your life.

Let's enjoy some of this new identity today—and talk about you and your special way as a cook. Who are you as a cook? What do you like to make? How would you describe the way you cook?

If it helps, pretend you're a chef who people love and now you are getting interviewed. Be yourself!

Now, your earliest memories with food. Write about some of them here, in sentences or bullet points:

Who cooked for you as a young child?

What were your favorite dishes and treats?

Your identity as a chef started long ago—with your earliest bites and creations. Your values, preferences, habits and CORE MEMORIES—all determine HOW you cook once you cook. What are your all-time favorite tasting foods? Name the foods or dishes, then name the qualities.

166

FAVORITE FOODS	THEIR QUALITIES

Circle and underline these qualities. These will be central parts of your identity as a cook as we move forward.

This week, when you prepare meals, bring some of these qualities into your cooking. And remember— no recipes! Keep practicing without them. You're doing great.

WEEK 5 / DAY FOUR
Cook using bread.

Most of us have bread in our kitchens, so let's use bread as our starting point today! Whether your bread is slightly staling or not—let's have fun!

You could make bread pudding, stuffing, croutons, or any other number of things. How to do these? Let's go over a couple.

Bread pudding is when you turn on the oven, tear this loaf up, drop it into a buttered baking dish, soak it to nearly its top with sweet delicious milk and eggs, throw in chopped fruits or berries, and stick it in the oven till it smells excellent and looks golden brown on the top. If it's on the wetter side at the end, that's cool. If it's on the dryer side, also awesome. You can't go wrong.

Stuffing also uses bread as its base, and you can either quick pulse process it in the food processor or leave the bread chunks whole. This will be a dryer as well as more savory ordeal. You'll want melted butter, and anything else delicious that you can see around the kitchen and envision deliciousness from. I love currants, apples, sausage-types and spicy green pepper and oyster types. You'll want to start with onions, and cook most of your tasty stuff in a pan first. The oven will serve the purpose of bringing it together.

Whatever you decide to do, your challenge today is to use your bread in a new way. If you're making croutons for a salad, think about what you'd want to do:

> Chop the bread up to little cubes. Toss them in oil, salt, and whatever spices you'd like, then put them in the oven at 375F or so until they're browning and getting crisp.

Have fun, and record the recipe of what you did below. Hey, you're getting better at this thing!

WEEK 5 / DAY FIVE
Make meatballs.

Meatballs are the easiest thing ever! To make them, you use your hands from beginning to end. Grab one big bowl, throw the meat in by unfolding the deli paper and turning it upside down (throw that out immediately and plan to toss the trash at the end of the day). You can use real meat or faux meat—both are great. Opt for ground. If you only have meat of some kind that's not ground—take out your food processor.

Once you have your meat in a bowl—add an egg—or not. As with anything, we're looking for deliciousness: chives, white onions, breadcrumbs, some tomato sauce, shredded parmesan. Whatever you do, make the batter consistent.

Form it into balls, trying not to overmix. You can cook them in a pan with oil, turning sometimes, in a pot immersed in broth or tomato sauce, or in the oven. Remember: the smaller the balls, the faster they'll cook.

When you smell something good, they're ready. How was that? Write about it here.

Now, before we go for the day, let's do an intentional **cleanup** together. We're doing a lot of cooking, which means your kitchen is getting a lot of action. Plan to do a deeper clean regularly.

> 1) Mark one day of your month on repeat in your calendar for a kitchen refresh.
>
> 2) Check out that chart you filled in earlier in our journey. If you haven't finished them all, do more today. For those of you who finished them, get in the kitchen and go through what needs a clean now.

Before you clean, let's all do a **5-7-8 breath** and I'll see you tomorrow for a longer-form challenge.

WEEK 5 / DAY SIX
Prepare to create a meal.

You've put time into your cooking—and you've put thought into your personal connection to cooking. Tomorrow, I want you to create a meal for others.

It could be just for yourself and a friend, or for a larger group. Think about the people who live with you. Don't they deserve a special meal? It will be fun. Today, we'll plan a bit.

Who's eating this meal?

And what's the setting for this meal experience—first your kitchen, then your dining room? You tell me. (Expand the picture.)

For our props—we'll play with ALL the foods and all the tools you have in your kitchen. Any specific ones come to mind? Foods you know are in there which you'd love to use for a special meal? Tools you want to pull out to use?

GATHER YOUR TRIBE

For the other characters at the table—I want you to INVITE them to tomorrow's meal, one by one. Jot your plan for inviting them down here.

Now, who are these people and what do they mean to you? Are they people who inspire you? Do they challenge you creatively when it comes to cooking? Write about them each here.

For me, as a chef, I had so many influences. I had my parents, who love food, both in different ways. I had my clients who were encouraging and also critical—made me get better, gave me cookbooks, showed me their tricks.

I had my friend Laura who insists that scones are ALL about the HEAVY CREAM. My grandma Mimi whose rice I told you about, my grandma on my other side who had Jello and Cool Whip ready when we came in late at night from a long road trip to see her (usually in the cold)—and countless others. My sister in law who is so British in her essence and so savvy about everything in the kitchen. My brother in law who makes the best of everything.

Who has influenced you on your cooking journey so far? Anyone recent?

And who have BEEN the other characters in THIS book? A supportive partner who has cheered you on and eaten everything as you cook? Has anyone been a co-star, your co-creator? Going on the creative journey with you? Any friends who are psyched you're cooking more? Write each person down and describe them in detail.

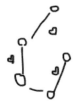

Of those who won't be with you in person tomorrow, choose one to join in spirit from afar— cook with that person in mind.

Tomorrow, we'll head into your kitchen to cook this special meal—with different parts and lots of love. Tonight, take extra loving care of yourself, adding in a bedtime ritual that will help you prepare for your big cooking day tomorrow.

My bedtime ritual   Yours?
                           Write one you love

Usually, shower, THEN dry brush,
Then oil up chin to toes w/
Apricot oil or almond oil
(whatever I have at the time)
Then brush my hair to stimulate
Scalp using Beneath Your Mask.

WEEK 5 / DAY SEVEN
Host a meal.

Today we're going to cook a meal and host a little group. To get you started: Make a drink and a dip.

Start with a big heap of sour cream, or a big heap of anything you have that's liquidy and would be a fun base (hummus, salsa, whatever you want). Go from there. Build on top of that one big heap, using your instinct. Enjoy the dip while you get into your cooking flow. The rest today is up to YOU.

When you're done with the evening, use this space as an end-of-night reflection from bed. How did the cooking feel? How were the group dynamics?

Use the next couple pages to write down your menu and describe the meal.

RAIN

W
O
O
P

179

WEEK SIX

THIS WEEK IS ABOUT FLEXING SOME MUSCLES, SHOWING YOURSELF WHAT YOU'VE GOT.

Every day will give you a unique challenge with an essential food item. Make THIS basic thing without recipes. Don't worry. I'll help you along the way! If you don't yet have a friend you're cooking with, this would be a good moment to invite someone along!

WEEK 6 / DAY ONE
Make mayo.

Mayo. I love it. It's a kitchen essential. Definitely something we'll want to be able to make on our own. To make mayo, there's one—no two—really essential ingredients.

First is **egg**. (Whole eggs or just the yolks.)

Second is **oil**—I like avocado oil but you can use any you have (just not a fragrant oil like coconut, and olive oil can get bitter when blending.)

Think about mayo—the taste. What else would you want to put in your food processor if you were planning to make it? Isn't there sort of a bright taste in there, too? CORRECT!

Some like adding lemon juice or vinegar (which helps to stabilize and also adds to the taste). Some like to use mustard (which can also be used to correct the mayo if it curdles).

Go get your food processor! Add the eggs first.

From there, add your mustard or your lemon juice if you're using it. Then slowly, in a fine drizzle, add your oil.

Go make a mayo—experiment—and write down any saucy recipes you come up with. You're on a roll!

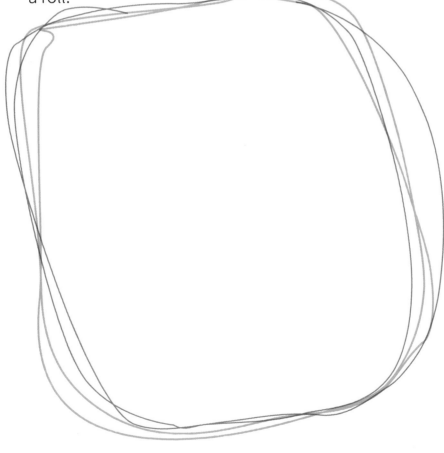

WEEK 6 / DAY TWO
Make overnight oats.

Today's challenge is overnight oats. In Germany and Switzerland, where this breakfast bowl originates, people call it "Bircher Muesli," and it's a super popular, non-fuss breakfast that's in little plastic or glass containers at coffee shops—where Starbucks might have their hard-boiled eggs.

To make it, take out a Tupperware and start adding tasty breakfast items such as oats, maybe some prepped granola, nuts of all kinds (even spiced nuts make for a good variation), dried fruits, honey, berries, bananas and stone fruits (chopped small), or chia seeds. If you have them—add chunks of orange or shredded apple. The mix is up to you!

Next, add a liquid that's creamy like yogurt or milk. Taste it as you sweeten. Add more milk if it's not wet enough. Put on the lid and enjoy it for the next two days or so.

Call them breakfast oats, overnight oats, Bircher Muesli—whatever you want. Think of this treat as really fun oatmeal that you eat cold. You don't necessarily need to leave them overnight in the fridge; a few hours will do. That's just a friendly name.

While you cook, write down your cute little recipe here. This is a nice one to save!

 (don't forget your cinnamon!)

WEEK 6 / DAY THREE
Make salad.

Today your challenge is to make a salad. A really good one. And, P.S., salads can be leaf-free.

Use what you have. No really, don't fuss. Almost anything goes well on top of salad greens. If you're using lighter weight greens like lettuce or spinach, keep your dressing to the side until you're ready to eat. If you're using kale, massage the dressing on with clean hands as soon as you finish the dressing.

Do you have any dressings you love making? Record them here.

Most of the liquids you'll come up with in your kitchen won't have names or a recipe associated, but dressings are basically an oil and some kind of acid, with the bonus of adding an emulsifier (something to make them creamy).

DRESSING = OIL + ACID + EMULSIFIER

Most dressings I make by hand with a fork to mix, but if the blender's out and in use, I might make a salad dressing for the week. One of my favorite starts to a dressing if I have the food processor out is—shallots, garlic, oil, vinegar or citrus, and then anything else you want. If you're using olive oil, do the other ingredients first then add the olive oil pulsing to keep it from getting bitter.

As you make your dressing, enjoy yourself during the process by tasting and adjusting.

Adjusting—an important word when it comes to cooking. There will be times when—oops!—you accidentally throw in a huge lump of salt or way too much cayenne pepper. In most cases, you'll want to add a neutral-tasting food item like broth or bread crumbs (in the case of dressing, oil or mayo), or, even just water, to get things back on track.

Taste what you're making until you feel you're realigned. (With baking batters, if you add too much baking soda, for instance, you can always add more milk or flour, increasing the overall volume of what you're making.) Adjusting—yes.

LET'S MAKE A DRESSING TOGETHER.

In general, dressings start with olive oil. Then, you add something acidic, bright and light like lemons, vinegar, grapefruit, capers juice—whatever you'd like. If it's bright to you, it's bright to a salad. If you're using vinegar, you can use white or red vinegar, sherry vinegar or apple cider vinegar (or balsamic and rice vinegar, which are lower in acidity.) Many options!

Want a creamy dressing? Emulsify it. That process begins with just oil and lemon. To add to this effect, use a mustard or anything else that's already creamy in your fridge. It could be chipotle mayo, avocado, or even egg yolk. These ingredients will add richness.

As you go, taste until you like the mixture by dropping or tapping the fork onto the back of your hand (It's generally cleaner than your palms or fingers!)

It's nice to keep certain combos in mind when dressing a salad (or marinating a steak, for that matter) so here are a few flavor profiles to consider:

A peanut lime dressing combines things like chili pepper flakes, lime, peanut butter, sesame oil, red onion, garlic and nuts—peanuts or cashews. Anything else you'd like to put in this realm of ingredients?

Caesar dressing is usually mashed garlic and anchovies, lemon and an egg yolk that you'll whisk while adding olive oil, and grated Parmesan. But I've made Caesar-like dressings using none of that. Can you think of how you might make one?

What dressing is going to come out of your kitchen today? Write down your recipe and enjoy your salad!

WEEK 6 / DAY FOUR
Make a dip.

Last week, you made a dip. Dips are so useful, everyone loves them, and I'm sure you do too. Today, your challenge is to make a signature dip. To get your juices flowing and keep it low key, let's go over two of the most basic beloved dips in the world.

Guacamole. Guacamole comes from a love of avocados. No, really. It's all about that love. Do you love avocados? The recipe—your recipe—will emerge from your love of them. Start with mashed avocado and smashed garlic as your base. If you leave out the garlic, no problem!

From there, see what you have that can be cut up small: chopped peppers, lime, lemon, corn, white onion, red onion, sour cream, mango, strawberry even! If you think it might taste good, it probably will. Keep tasting as you add and keep the salt and pepper grinders handy.

Hummus. In its most traditional form, hummus is chickpeas, garlic (raw or roasted), tahini, and lemon—combined. If you can get a garlic paste somewhere, that's a great shortcut. If you don't have chickpeas, white or beige beans work well, too. Tahini is just ground sesame seeds, so if you have sesame seeds, but no tahini, you can start by toasting them and pasting those up in the processor and adding a big glug of olive oil and salt.

For variation, blend in roasted beets or roasted red peppers. If you want your hummus to be spicy, add harissa or chili paste. To serve, be creative. Drizzle it with olive oil, green pumpkins seeds, red pepper flakes or salt.

Today, go make a dip. Start with that first base ingredient—beans, or avocado—and get that part mashed into dip texture. From there, experiment and try as often as you want.

Enjoy it and have fun! See you tomorrow to pull out your blender and make smoothies.

WEEK 6 / DAY FIVE
Make a smoothie.

Today—make a smoothie. I know, it's so healthy, right? Let's do it. I'll do one over here too. Here's the thing—smoothies can be made of so much different stuff. You don't need to buy them out and about. You can make them at home. Today, let's celebrate that fact! Now—let's get to our smoothies.

Smoothies use all fruits, vegetables, nuts, nut butters, waters (like coconut water) and more. I think the big key to making them good is to make sure you're adding a smoothing ingredient like a banana, yogurt, avocado, or coconut cream.

You can add lots of things you find healthy: oats, flaxseeds, oat bran, wheat germ, chia seeds, yogurt, plums, apples, kiwis. That, for instance, would be a good smoothie with bananas.

Alright, y'all! Get to it. Make a smoothie.

WEEK 6 / DAY SIX
Make frittata.

Today let's make frittata, one of the easiest, most rewarding baked goods around. It's like quiche without crust. Turn your oven to 350F, or 400F if you're in a rush. Pull out those eggs—this dish is primarily eggs, so you'll want to use five or six eggs maybe.

Frittata "batter" is liquidy, eggs and milk, with some fillings throughout.

Let's get started on the fillings. Start with onions and/or garlic in your skillet. The onions and garlic give frittatas their characteristic yumminess, so try not skipping both. Watery vegetables like peppers, zucchinis, etc. work well and are quick to cook up.

While that stuff is on the pan, whisk up your eggs and some milk with a fork in a bowl. The eggs are your binder. They will hold everything together.

If you want to throw in grated cheese, salt or pepper or other spices, throw them into that eggy mix.

Once the veggies in the pan have cooked enough that they're starting to smell good in your kitchen, dump them into your buttered baking dish of choice (pie pan great) and let them cool for a bit.

Pour the egg mixture in when you're ready.

If you need more egg liquid in order for the veggies to be immersed, add milk or anything else that's dairy, like ricotta or heavy cream, even a little yogurt which tangs it up—to the egg mixture.

If you want more color last minute, throw in some spinach or chard. It will wilt right down in the frittata and make for a beautiful scene.

Can you think of any foods that rhyme with frittata?

If you have bread and prefer to make stratta—think about this—stratta is layers of bread, egg poured over, include vegetables, about an hour in the oven.

Did you make your frittata? By the way—you can make frittata in the oven or on the stove, but I'm sure you've inferred that. If you cook it in a cast iron skillet on the stove, some people would cover the dish up so it cooks evenly. You could start with the veggies in the skillet and then just pour in the egg mix—one pan deal.

Great. With your skills today, you're able to make quiche as well as frittata. (Frittata traditionally doesn't include cream, just the eggs and vegetables and maybe cheese—whereas quiche typically always include milk, cream and eggs.)

WEEK 6 / DAY SEVEN
Make crust.

Today, we'll go over how to make crust. To start, let's return to our batter spectrum.

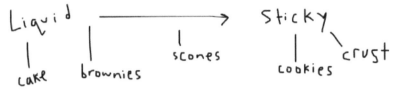

Crusts are even thicker than cookie batter—and ideally a little bouncier—and we'll want to refrigerate that dough before we get it going in the oven. I start with fat. It's one of those rare cases where you want to start with cold butter.

Dice up a cold bar of butter. Put any kind of flour in there. Mix—more like it, mash. Add salt or sugar if you want. Then, prepare a cup of ice water. An ice cube or two in a glass of water. From there, I just pour in little bits at the time and keep mashing the dough with my hands until it's in a good shape—sticking together, pretty smooth.

Next, wrap it into a ball in saran wrap.

197

In 20 minutes—or two hours, take it out and good to go.

Press it into a pie dish or anything else, and give it a few minutes baking before adding fillings—whatever you want. Hope you make something great, and I'll see you tomorrow—the start of week seven.

Draw what you made today here.

WEEK SEVEN

YOU'RE REALLY COOKING.

This is our second to last week together, and I'm so excited for what's ahead. You might be tired, and that's okay! This week will be a combination of reflection, writing and cooking.

WEEK 7 / DAY ONE
Check in with your body.

Let's start this week with a body check-in. And also—let me just say, in the quiet of these pages—you're amazing. You've gotten so far! Welcome to your week seven.

Now let's talk about your body. I want you to pay attention to it while you cook. The more you cook, the more I want you to notice it because those motions will become repetitive. It's better to notice things now, and correct a little early on rather than years from now. These moves become your groove. If you've been cooking daily for years, use today to stop and notice, making changes where you see room for improvement.

If you're carrying a heavy pan, don't use just one hand. Use the second hand to support the base (while wearing an oven glove!).

Don't force yourself to be fast. Take your time and let your speed increase naturally over time. In commercial kitchens, where people are cooking on the clock, there are lots of cuts and burns. In your own private kitchen, there's none of this pressure. You may be a busy person, but you have the luxury of a domestic setting and doing things on your own terms.

Relish this. Take your time, breathe, and drink a soothing beverage—tea, wine, whatever you'd like—when you cook.

Today's cooking challenge to start the week?

Go into the kitchen and make anything that you'd like. But watch your body in the process—how it moves when you take out the trash, when you open cupboards, when you lift things. Try out different moves and see what you may want to change.

WEEK 7 / DAY TWO
Share your recommendations.

Today, I want you to act as if close friends
are visiting while you're out of town, and
you're making a map for them to enjoy your
neighborhood, city or town. Where would you send
them?! Which restaurants, bars, cafes, bakeries,
grocery stores, or other amazing stops? Draw a
map or list them here—that's the first half of your
challenge for the day.

MY FAVORITE SPOTS IN

Now, prepare these imaginary friends a quick dessert to place on the table when they walk in to your home. That's what your cooking challenge will be today: **raw dessert truffles**—an essential skill for life and an excellent, easy homecoming gift of many varieties.

Covered in powder like simple cacao powder, or pressed with goji berries or edible flowers, they feel so unique and fancy. But the process could not be simpler.

First, get out the food processor. Or, if you don't have one, use your blender. You'll just need to get in there and stir a bit in between these steps.

Throw in a big heap of nuts—any kind like almonds or hazelnuts. Next, find some dry fruit, dates or dried apricots and add those in. At this point, if you just mixed that up, you would have something sticky enough to turn into balls.

Now, with a base intact, think supplements such as flax seeds, chia seeds, hemp seeds, another kind of nut, superfood powders—and add what you like.

Take the lid off the food processor, remove the blade, and start shaping little balls. Prepare a bowl of tasty powder to roll them in, like ground coconut or matcha powder. Chill them in the refrigerator or leave them on the counter.

How did that go? Draw what you made and label some of the ingredients!

WEEK 7 / DAY THREE
Deepen v. Define.

Today we're going to explore the difference between defining and deepening. The key is understanding the influence of whatever you're adding.

For example, let's say you add a spice to a dish. It will either be flavor-defining or flavor-deepening. So what's the difference? In the first case, it becomes dominant. The name of spice may even appear in whatever you call the dish.

With deepening, you're adding richness that affects the overall impact of the dish through collaboration with other layers. In this case, its flavor is there—but only slightly.

Let's take cookies as an example, starting with only neutral ingredients like eggs, flour, milk, and sugar. At that point, you add a quarter bottle of cinnamon. As long as your volumes are standard, the cinnamon will not only contribute to the project but will define the project.

As long as your batter tastes like cinnamon (in a pleasant way), you'll probably end up calling these "cinnamon cookies." What a contribution this little spice can make!

On the other hand, if you threw that same amount of cinnamon into a pot of developing stew, it wouldn't alter the taste of the whole stew significantly, but it will add depth and complexity.

This is deepening. If you taste your stew very closely, you might taste that spice, but it won't be the first thing you notice.

Time for your challenge today! Pick an ingredient. **Make two things.** With one, use the ingredient to "define" the dish, and in the other use the ingredient to "deepen" it. This will require some creativity so give yourself some time to go for it. Start with one or the other, but do both.

See you tomorrow!

WEEK 7 / DAY FOUR
Make fish or chicken.

What do you have in your kitchen, meat and fish eaters? Fish or chicken? I hope you have one or the other. Today, let's explore one or the other. I'm going to go over both, and put a challenge at the end of this day for vegetarians.

TWO TIPS THAT APPLY TO BOTH FISH AND CHICKEN

Marinades always help! A marinade is a tasty liquid (that you've created out of a few liquids) which the fish or chicken can sit in at room temperature for a half hour or so. Any marinades you love making?

Get that thing to room temp! Don't cook straight from the fridge. Let it come to room temp first by sitting it on the counter for an hour or more.

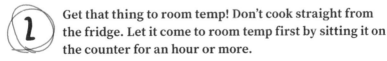

Now—fish!

Don't be afraid of fish! When in doubt—drizzle it with butter and lemon, put it in the oven, and done! Foil is nice because it keeps the moisture in. I use lower heats in general—350F and 300F. But let's start from the beginning. In general, at the store you'll run into two kinds of fish:

1) **Delicate fillets** like sole or flounder, which turn opaque when they're cooked. You can either cook these low and slow, or you can sear them on the pan quickly, which brings a crispness to the outside while preserving the juiciness inside.

2) **Thicker fish steaks** like salmon and swordfish, which we don't want to overcook. One of my favorite ways to cook salmon—learned from my brother in law—is to make a marinade of olive oil, Dijon mustard, soy sauce, honey, garlic and salt and pepper.

Set the salmon in the oven at 350F, paint on the marinade, and then every few minutes, continue to paint more marinade onto the fish. So delicious and it stays so soft! You can change that marinade up, too. Just make sure there's something sweet in it.

I love getting a whole fish, like sea bass and red snapper, scaled and gutted but with the head and tail left on. I only ever do one thing with these: Set the oven to 400F, put the fish in a pan and spend a few minutes dressing it up with good stuff like herbs, garlic, salt, and so on—maybe even stuffing a bit into the inside as well.

Once in the oven, I check on it about a half-hour later. These are so fun because you put a whole fish out on the table in the same pan it cooked in.

Then we've got **shrimp**. Chefs often cook shrimp unshelled in oil, adding garlic after a bit. Or, you could boil the unshelled shrimp briefly instead. Personally, I don't like to unshell shrimp during my meal, so I'll unshell prior to serving.

Let's review **tuna** salad (yep, that could be you today)! There's not much to it: mayo, tuna (from the can!) and then fun stuff like celery, Worcester sauce, red onion, capers—whatever you want.

Speaking of cans, anchovies and sardines are great. All those Omega 3 fatty acids for such a low price? Amazing! Get them and use them. They require no cooking and have all the health benefits of fresh fish. Go for fancier ones if you can, because they will have been more respectfully packaged.

Eat them whole on their own in bowls, or use anchovies in salad dressing like for a classic Caesar or a Puttanesca tomato sauce!

Finally, let's not forget about **mussels**—my favorite thing to order at restaurants and so easy to make for yourself at home too. Start by cleaning them with a good rinse in the sink. Then, make a delicious broth using wine, celery, butter and whatever else you'd like such as tomatoes and garlic, or bits of other sauces. Place the mussels in the sauce and cover the pot. You know they're ready when they've opened up. Pair with a crusty bread and devour!

What are your favorite ways to cook any of the seafood items I just went through briefly? What comes to mind? Write here!

On to Poultry—today chicken!

My favorite way to deal with chicken (say breasts) is to simply take it out of its packaging and handle it. I wash it, dry it, place it on a sheet of wax paper (gloopy side down) and turn the oven to 350F. Maybe I'll add some salt and pepper. Then, I'll set an alarm for 30 minutes, take it out and let it cool. Finally, I'll use my hands to shred it into pieces.

If you're working with a **whole chicken**, roast it breast side down. This helps to protect the delicate white meat as well as enhances it thanks to the weight and succulence of everything above it dripping down. When you're roasting whole birds of any kind, find kitchen string and tie the structure up so that it's compact. You want its parts to huddle and collaborate, rather than spread out and dry. One tie from neck to wings, and then another stringing the wings together. Make sense?

Now, what do you think will happen if you put the whole chicken into your oven, uncovered? If you imagined it would dry out a bit, you're right. So that's what we avoid when we put our birds breast side down.

When it comes to cooking times, leave it in for about 40 minutes at 350F. If you want the breast browned, you can flip it. Poke the thickest part, which is most often the thigh, and if no blood comes out, take it out. You can also poach a chicken, which means to bring a pot of some liquid (broth) to boil then cover the pot with the chicken in it for 45 minutes.

If you have a half-eaten or pre-bought roasted chicken in the fridge, use your hands to tear it apart—and be aggressive. The squeamish miss out on lots of good meat by avoiding a full pick through. Put all the good meat you find in a Tupperware. (No bones, though!)

To make **fried chicken**, mix a bowl of flour, salt, pepper, and some other granulated spices for flavor. First, dip the chicken in a bowl of egg, then coat the chicken in the flour mix and immerse the parts in hot boiling oil until they fry up gloriously.

To make **chicken nuggets**, ground up raw chicken thighs in the food processor, make mounds, dip in egg and panko breadcrumbs, and bake at 425F for about 6 minutes on each side or until brown.

For turkeys, ducks, and geese all the same general rules apply. Plus, your instinct. That's the key here. Do what you want!

What are your favorite ways to cook fish or chicken? Write here!

For today's cooking challenge, try a new way of cooking! If you need help from your crew, ask for it! You're doing great.

For vegetarians!

Cook from parts to whole. You've been rocking it this week! Let's ease off and go back to basics. One nice way to go about cooking is very intuitive—and that's what we'll practice today: it's making sure every part is delicious for the whole dish to be delicious.

I do this all the time. For example, if I'm making a lentil salad, I'll boil the lentils, cool them off under the faucet with cold water, then toss them in salt and oil. At that point, I'll taste the lentils and make sure they're delicious. They'll sit there in a bowl while I continue on with other parts.

Then, I'll do the same for other ingredients: I'll salt and pepper the chopped hard boiled eggs and toss them with olive oil. I'll salt and toast the nuts on the stove. Once all these pieces are tasty enough in their own right (meaning, after you try one bite you immediately want another), then you combine them.

This is how you make a whole dish delicious: separately. Each part is delicious on its own.

214

Ready for your **cooking challenge**?

Go to your kitchen to prepare a dish. It could be anything, but start to compose it with this idea of parts in mind. Making each part delicious, seasoned, tasting it, before moving on to the next. Then combine, eat, ponder and jot down how it all made you feel.

WEEK 7 / DAY FIVE
Draw and color.

Today let's take a break from cooking and draw! What will be draw? FRUITS AND VEGETABLES. I'll write some notes on different ones, and you do your best to draw them.

Ginger. Scrape off most of the skin with a spoon so you won't lose the meat.

Chilis. The seeds are the spiciest part, so include them in your chop if you want heat, and core the chili and chop only the flesh if you don't.

Whole corn on the cob. Stand it in a Tupperware or on top of a sauté pan and shear it right out into the receptacle.

Garlic. Every time I roast something in the oven, I try to throw a few cloves in the center of the pan, skin still on. When they come out, the garlic skin slips off quickly and out comes juicy roasted garlic, which you can use on anything—even just buttered toast.

Cauliflower. Boil it in a vinegar-based brine to get it pickley.

Avocados. They're healthiest near the skin, where the flesh is darker. That's their immune system, where they defend against intruders. When you're adding avocado to a dish, nourish yourself by scraping those last bits at the skin with your spoon.

Cucumbers. To soften them, salt them once they're sliced and let them sit.

Mashed potatoes. Try boiling them, removing the skin and mashing them with a fork instead of a food processor. Then, put the chunks in a saucepan on low heat and slowly incorporate butter. Once it's off the heat, thin it out and give it an extra support of creaminess by adding some milk, cream or half & half. The same treatment applies for all root vegetables: sweet potatoes, parsnips, turnips, and so on.

Apples. The healthiest apples are the green ones. If you want to lose a little weight, or just feel in good balance, get a bag of them and eat regularly. They're also excellent for liver and skin health.

Cherries. When they're in season, buy them. They'll make you happy—promise!

Berries. A wise investment every time they're on sale. Blackberries, blueberries, raspberries, strawberries. The darker the better. These are some of the highest real estate value food items in the world. So many antioxidants. Truly like multivitamins.

Grapefruit. I personally don't like the taste, but I do use it medicinally in combination with caffeine to boost the impact of caffeine if I'm really tired. Try it. It works!

Figs. Beautiful, luxurious, elegant fruit. I love them with any kind of dairy or faux dairy, like yogurt or sour cream, and some honey. I'll even just eat them fresh, on my way out the door.

Lemons. I drink lemon water daily, starting in the morning and throughout the day. My favorite thing to do is to add pink Himalayan salt to the pitcher, or some warm water. It neutralizes some of the acidity and restores minerality in your body first thing upon waking.

Papaya. They will always remind me of living in India, when I'd ride my dirt bike home with groceries and a papaya in between my legs. The seeds are great if you need a cleanse. Do your research, but it's good to know that they're there if you need them.

Plantains. Slice them like a banana and fry them in coconut oil before serving them with beans and brown rice. Heaven.

Watermelon. My favorite way to slice them is to make wedges and create handles.

Now you add your own! What are your favorite fruits and veggies? List and draw them here. Add notes! When do you like to eat them, and why?

WEEK 7 / DAY SIX
Cook Meat or Faux Meat.

Welcome back! You are doing so great. Let's dive into meat.

One way to work with meat is to decide whether the cut you have is tough or tender and to choose your cooking method accordingly.

If it's tender, like most good steaks, you'll want to cook it quickly and with harsh heat. The thicker and tougher a cut is, the longer you'll want to cook it and the more you'll want to consider a marinade.

Overall, with meats, you're essentially caretaking. You're watching out for them. You're adding to them. You're spending time with them and adjusting their progress.

It's important to let meat come to room temperature before cooking it. And the same goes for after it's done. Let meats rest before slicing or eating.

If you have a big piece of meat, like a rib roast or pork roast, take it out of the fridge and salt it the moment you're going to use it. The bigger, the earlier. What are your insights around meat?

When it comes to braising, it can be done with all kinds of liquids. A pot roast uses gradual cooking in a delicious juice that makes the meat tender. Or, you can cook smoked ham at a lower temperature for a long time in Madeira wine, for instance. If you have lamb shanks, you could put them in some water with a bunch of tasty herbs thrown in, and cook it down until the liquid has evaporated.

Sometimes, in a pan, I'll brown a piece of meat, then reduce the temperature and add liquid. It gives the meat texture and makes the liquid richer.

To test the doneness when cooking, always poke or slice into the thickest part and check the color with your eyes.

Every piece of meat is a little different, and that's where your senses come in: you can see and feel everything you need to know.

Most people want to eat lamb when it's pink, and not when it's overcooked. For pork roast, which starts off as pink, you'll most likely want to eat it moist and white. Either way, experiment and get to know how you, your friends or your family wants to eat things.

Basting is rarely a bad thing. That's when you pour fat and juices over the meat while it's cooking. The downside of this is that every time you open the oven to do this you're letting the heat out.

Thanksgiving turkeys taste good from a brine or dry cure. What's that, you ask? For a brine, you'll want ice cold water with a good balance of sugar and salt of some kind that have dissolved. You can brine a frozen turkey for a week if it's covered!

Tenderizing something is physically breaking down the tendons in a piece of meat. For instance, you can pound veal scallops to tenderize them. You could also, for that matter, tenderize a piece of chard by pounding the veins down to break them or massage them with coconut oil. The mouth likes things broken down. It makes chewing and digestion easier.

When it comes to marinades, your imagination is the limit. But, in general, the tougher and bigger a piece of meat, the more you'll want to care for it, salt it, marinate it, slow cook it, etc.

OK. Let's talk about faux meat. I love Beyond Burger. I grill their patties and eat them with avocado mayo, ketchup and juicy heirloom tomatoes on brioche buns with a side salad sitting in the garden and I feel like a queen! People love Impossible, too. These gateway brands are opening the door for more artisan options!

Today, cook some kind of meat, faux or animal. Enjoy yourself and write any of your favorite processes below, or one you discover today:

WEEK 7 / DAY SEVEN
Make a liquid. Any liquid.

Humans like sweetness, saltiness, fattiness, and brightness. When you're trying to make something as bitter as spinach taste so good you can't stop eating it, you're going to want to add all that to it— no holding back.

And, generally, that tastiness comes from a liquid.

The process of building liquids is all the same, from sauces to soups to dressings to smoothies or braises for mushrooms and fish. There's so much to choose from so let's explore just a few aspects of this topic today before getting to the cooking.

Most liquids can be reused quite easily, so think about what you have as a starting point. Cooked scallops, for instance, leave a delicious, sweet oil behind that can be the base for something else. Even if something is not outright delicious, like, say, the water you used to boil broccoli, it's still fortified above plain water. Use it to cook or substantiate something else like beans or as the water base of a soup.

Deglazing something, aka, getting sticky bits off a pan and into a new delicious liquid, can be done using wine, cream, orange juice, water—whatever you want.

HOW TO DEGLAZE:

Turn the heat up briefly to get all that stuff broken down into each other. Use this to create a sauce or to stimulate the start of a new project. For instance, let's say you've sautéed some vegetables and there's stuff sticking to the bottom of the pan you used.

Go ahead and add a liquid to your pan, then bring the heat back on to integrate everything. Taste, adjust and voila! That could be the start of your liquid project today.

In general, if you want to achieve smoothness when working with liquids, use the blender. Be careful with blending hot things, though. The blades heat up extremely fast and can cause all the food to erupt. If you're blending soup, add small portions at a time, opening the lid to allow it to cool in between.

There are all kinds of delicious liquids you can make—and I'm going to remind you of one of my favorites —a sweet one! Especially if you have a group around.

Whipped cream. First, take out a bowl of ice and sit another bowl inside it. Combine heavy cream, a little sugar, maybe a little vanilla, and whip, whip, whip. It will get there. It's fun to pass around at a party, or back and forth between you and a friend.

Whatever you make today, give it a name here, and a brief description—**as if it's on a menu**!

(See you tomorrow for the start of week eight— our last week together!)

WEEK EIGHT

IT'S WEEK EIGHT—I CAN HARDLY BELIEVE IT. HOW FAR YOU'VE COME.

We'll do a mix of all the things we've practiced together—and you'll be stretched to work in new ways with food. Before we begin our official final week, take a moment to write down some of the things you've learned while on this journey.

1.

2.

3.

4.

5.

WEEK 8 / DAY ONE
Get spiritual.

In yoga, there's a phrase, "holding space." That the teacher's job is to "hold the space" for the students, who are having their own unique, authentic, organic experiences. That's one way to think of food, and I want you to work with this premise of holding space as you cook today (if only for a moment, to see how the idea shifts your mind.)

What I've found is that food has its own opinions: the way it wants to be handled, what other ingredients it wants to be assembled among, and so on. Today, as you cook, consider your role as gently guiding its mission, or its purpose.

Let's take a practical example—**tomatoes**.

SOME TOMATOES ARE FIRM AND WOULD BE GREAT IN A SANDWICH (USUALLY THOSE ARE BEEFSTEAKS), WHILE SOME NEED HEAT (LIKE PLUMS OR ROMAS) AND ARE HAPPIEST TO BE MADE INTO A SAUCE. OTHERS, LIKE HEIRLOOMS (ESPECIALLY AT THEIR PEAK) ARE SO PERFECT, ALL THEY NEED IS SOME SALT—ANYTHING ELSE WOULD BE A DISSERVICE TO THEM.

It really is an existential thing to ponder: that a fruit's life, a fish's life, has a purpose. It has a way it wants to express itself. Consider this today: You are only there to aid its purpose.

This knowing; this sensitive listening—being in service to the lifeform in your hands—is one way to think about cooking. If you act deliberately and think of food as living "beings," like yourself, you'll find you enjoy it that much more.

Many cooking principles emerge from sensitivity and thoughtfulness. Which living thing doesn't want to be cleaned appropriately, or wouldn't like to come to room temperature before being thrown into extreme heat? Can you think of any other principles that come from treating food with care for the lives of the plants and animals in your hands?

Here's the cooking challenge for today.

Go into your kitchen and pick up a fruit, vegetable, nut, or anything else that's unprocessed. Hold it in your hands and observe it. Then, ask yourself: What does this thing want? How would it like to be treated? How can I honor its life in my next steps? You don't need answers right away. Take your time—the food will lead you.

Go to your kitchen to experiment! Record any of your insights here:

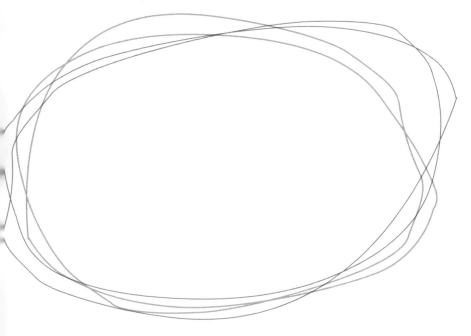

WEEK 8 / DAY TWO
Let the kitchen feed the home.

As someone who loves the kitchen and is familiar with its tools and ingredients, you're in a privileged position to make all KINDS of things based on what's inside it.

Today—your challenge is to extend your kitchen into your home, to use the practical ingredients within it to nurture other aspects of your life aside from eating. Here are some ideas of things that I make on a regular basis that begin in the kitchen and end up in another room.

Apple cider vinegar hair rinse— I'm a fan and tester of beauty products, but one of my all-time favorite ways to return my hair to childlike softness and cleanliness comes straight out of the kitchen. In a plastic tub of any kind (usually I use yogurt tubs), I fill apple cider vinegar and about the same amount of water. I sit the tub near my shower and, about once a week or every two weeks, I dump the container over my head, massage it in, and let

235

it sit on my scalp for ten minutes. Try it. It works wonders.

A nutritious gum rinse—I make a mouthwash / oil pulling oil for myself that I use daily. I make it out of any oil (olive oil or avocado oil, or any other edible oils that are liquid at room temperature and whose taste you like.) I mix in a few essential oils that are safe for mouths—peppermint, clove, lemon. Sometimes I add a little Apple Cider Vinegar for all of its benefits.

I put it in my bathroom in a little bottle with my own label. I use it before I brush my teeth in the morning. Google 'oil pulling' and try it yourself. You don't need to swish for 20 minutes. Just as long as you can! I do a little bit of time—whatever I want— but I do it daily. Before brushing.

RINSE { AVOCADO OIL, ESSENTIAL OILS. }

White sugar—I don't use white sugar often in my cooking, but sometimes it ends up in my kitchen because someone brings it for a party or another member of my household buys it. When it is hanging around, I fill an old yogurt container up (again, plastic containers are better than glass—for when they accidentally fall.) I put it in the shower, and most days—when I'm using body wash, I mix some of the sugar in to my palm with the soap and scrub. If you do it regularly, it makes your skin shiny and soft.

I'll stop there, but I use kitchen supplies for many things. Today, your challenge is to make something out of your kitchen that ends up being useful in another room of your house.

What other ideas come to mind? Record what you make here.

WEEK 8 / DAY THREE
Create a common thread.

Often I feel the best meals have a little bit of something in common throughout every dish. So for instance, a certain kind of milk, or a broth, that goes into everything you make—from the string beans to the fish to the little dessert squares. This way, all the dishes are connected—in a way you can't place, in a subconscious way.

The result is romantic. It becomes a journey, a story with some of the same characters carrying through. It might be imperceptible, but it's felt.

Today, see how you can carry an aspect of one dish into the next. Make a full meal. Use the leftover liquid from sautéing something as the base for boiling something else, or making a sauce for a next course.

Write this meal down here—recording what ingredients you used and how much. Instead of just writing this down, take pictures. Make a fuller recording of this one.

Remember, a 'little bit' or a 'lot' are fine if you'd prefer that to 'a teaspoon of' or 'a cup of.' Let your language be free. You're writing another menu.

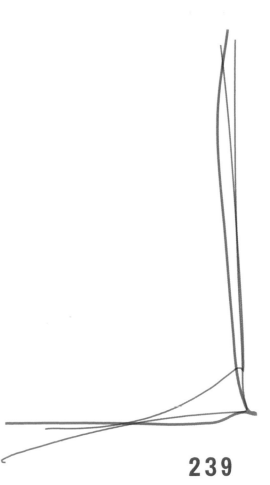

WEEK 8 / DAY FOUR
Move around.

Cooking is a kinetic, physical experience of creativity; a mix of creating things, observing things, tasting things, finding things, and more. When you keep yourself in motion, you gain insight and find items you'd like to bring into the process.

Today, as you cook, focus on keeping your movement in flow. When you're out of ideas for a moment, clean up. While you put objects back in the fridge or wipe down cabinets, you'll encounter something that throws you back into creative mode.

Movement is more than just your body moving throughout the space of your kitchen. It's also the movement of food from one day to the next.

As cooks, we don't usually start from scratch every time we cook. **Instead, we use what's in the kitchen, what began days ago**, condiments and extra bits of former meals that have sat dutifully in your fridge.

You might steam broccoli one day and end up using it in a stir-fry the next—or use a super spicy salsa from takeout on Monday to deepen a chili you're making on Friday. If I make a big batch of quinoa, I'll save some of it in a container to use on something else. And if I brew a pot of tea or coffee, I pour some into a jar and enjoy it the next day chilled.

MANTRA
i embrace change.
i notice how many parts of time and space
collaborate to help me in the present moment.

Today's challenge: Go to your kitchen and look for something that's nearly finished—available in a small amount. Use that as a starting point for a new dish. Keep moving as you build on it with ingredients you find, and things you make. This is the kinetic feeling of cooking.

WEEK 8 / DAY FIVE
Cook by layering.

Many dishes, like lasagna, moussaka (like Greek lasagna) and an infinite number of delicious others that may not have a name, are an act of layering.

The freedom to substitute is a central feature to the layering process. For example, you can commit to making lasagna if you know you have lasagna noodles and tomato-y anything (could even just be ketchup!) From there, you have freedom.

All layers taste good individually—make sure of this, and you will have a scrumptious layered dish.

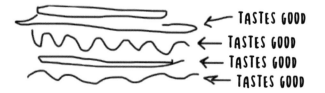

400F—get the idea on the horizon. From knowing you have lasagna noodles—look around. If you have garlic or onions, that's a nice start. None of that? Consider creams. Build your sauce on the stove—in a skillet or a pot. The important thing is to make the sauce or sauces you use taste good to you too. In layered dishes, a nice (salty enough) delicious sauce can help to make the whole thing delicious—even if some of the layers are simple, like spinach.

Today, make a layered dish. Use the oven. Keep combining and building until you love what you're tasting.

Consider tasty as well as neutral ingredients like broccoli—something that holds flavor well, but isn't a bang. With lasagna, the noodles are one of your neutrals, so you'll alternate, tasty sauce, neutral, tasty sauce, neutral.

If you have cheese, shred or slice and make a layer of it. That will help things to stick together.

No cheese? Whisk egg and pour it in. That does the same, though this will make it more of a casserole.

Either way, layer by layer you make lasagna, or casserole, or moussaka, or anything else—like I said, loads of things that don't have names.

Go for it and see you tomorrow!

Draw the layers here as you make them.

WEEK 8 / DAY SIX
Exploring crispiness.

Today, we'll explore what makes something crispy—and practice that. Crispiness comes from fat heating up and then cooling. It can also come from dryness, like dehydrating bananas in the oven or adding breadcrumbs to a bean burger patty. Any other ideas of how crispiness happens?

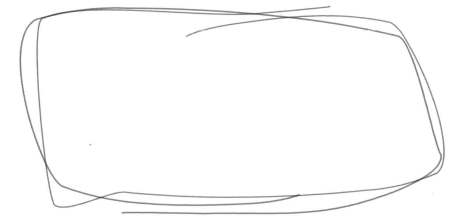

To make something crispy, you want to make the outsides fattier (more oil, higher heat.) Essentially, you want the outside to cook faster than the insides, either because of dryness or oiliness.

How would you cook the outsides faster than the insides? Write what you know here.

It's useful to know the **basic method for deep frying**, so let's go over it. Some people have deep friers at home, but most of us don't. We'll use a pot and lots of oil. Yes, deep frying will deplete your oil.

How to do it? First, fill a pot a quarter of the way up with a resilient oil like canola or grapeseed—not olive oil (too delicate). Bring it to a boil.

In the meantime, fill one mixing bowl with whisked egg and one bowl with flour. The flour bowl can also welcome salt and any dried spices.

Then, dip your item in egg, then in flour and then immerse it in boiling oil. There are techniques for making sure the flour is really coating all parts of the thing such as flattening between two pieces of parchment paper. But I'm here to encourage you to use your intuition to make changes and adjustments only you know you need.

So, today, your challenge is to fry something, or make something crispy. Essentially—play with this idea of crispiness, and enjoy eating what you make. Tomorrow—we're putting ALL of our lessons together.

WEEK 8 / DAY SEVEN
Prepare to party.

You did it! You got to the end of this journey. I hope you've learned more about yourself and cooking and that you're starting to feel absolutely comfortable cooking without recipes.

I want to thank you for allowing me to guide you—and welcome you to go back through this book and share some of your writing, drawings, and anything else you made in these pages with me. **#NOTACOOKBOOK**

To celebrate your journey, let's prepare a party.

It can be anything, in any time.

Small, big, outdoors, indoors, for strangers, for family, for you alone, for you and a loved one... the possibilities for feeding your soul as a host and giving love to others through food are endless.

Now that you're more practiced with your cooking, I want you to think of hosting as an essential part of

248

your life as a cook. And since this week marks the end of our time together, it's only natural to show what you've learned to others by having them over.

My final challenge to you will take you a few days, but I want to give you tips for making it happen, so we'll begin the planning process here together.

1. Theme, mood and guests

First order of business: decide what you're gifting. When you invite people over, you're gifting them a mood, a sense of comfort, energy, cause for celebration. So, let's start with a theme and overall ambience—then get into the guest list.

HOW TO CHOOSE YOUR THEME AND MOOD: I've hosted Halloween parties with surprise murder mysteries sprung upon guests; cozy, plaid-and-knit autumn parties in time for Thanksgiving; and and most recently a birthday party where I recreated the theme of my childhood: trolls with hair you can mold, heart candies with love phrases on them, dim lighting, red tinsel, '80s-vibe love music, and party favors with small unicorn notebooks and mechanical pencils in them! Use your imagination and enjoy yourself. It's an experience! It's you!

What kind of party will you throw this time? Draw pictures, and sketch out your idea here. What food will you serve? What music will you play? Who will you invite? How will people feel? Once you've jotted ideas down for both theme and mood, add your guests. If it feels more natural to start with guests, do that and go back!

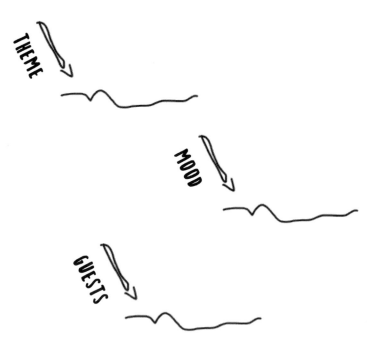

2. Menu Planning

What food will you serve? If you need ideas, browse some of the challenges we went through together! If you're cooking for just a few people, perhaps you want to go for something very elegant like mussels or a whole baked fish with a delicate dessert like a crumble with this season's peak fruit.

If you're cooking for a bunch of people, maybe you want to ask guests to bring something specific like a loaf of bread or nice wine to go with your hearty food like a chili, pasta, tacos or big bowls of salads.

One idea to spark your imagination is... If you were going to throw a party for ten people right now, and not run out to the grocery store, what would you make? Go into your kitchen and explore! Get an idea and write it below.

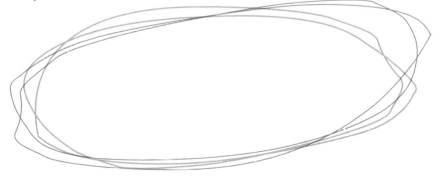

3. Delegate

As you get closer to your party, let dinner guests bring some of the goods! Why? Because they will ask what you need or want so tell them! It's one of my favorite fringe things about hosting. Your kitchen is immediately full again!

So, when someone texts you asking what they can bring, be specific. If you can't think of specifics, think of something you always need more of like lemons or even basic butter!

What do you bring when you're a guest? Name and draw some of the things you've brought to parties over the years.

4. Design, Decor & Atmosphere

Party favors are not just for kids parties, though that's where I learned them—and I love them as an adult too. They make parties super special.

What guest doesn't like to wander to the train or back to their car holding a bouquet of flowers or a little satchel of a cutely packed homemade bar of some kind?

As a host, you can prepare little party favors with just a batch of brownies or granola bars, some tissue paper and string. It could even be a chance to show off a friend's product if, say, you know someone who makes chocolate bars or bracelets. What a nice thing to do that delights everyone.

Draw a party favor that comes to your imagination. It could be a bag filled with things, or a single item.

5. On the day of—introduce a learning opportunity.

Beyond just cooking for your guests and inviting them into your home, by hosting you also have the opportunity to introduce them to new foods—things that you love and feel they'll love, too.

On the day of or day before, go out and get an ice cream you really love that not many of your friends are likely to know, or ask people to come over and cook with you. It's such a great feeling to learn something new by coming over to cook at someone's house.

When you're done and the house is cleaned up, tell me—did that feel like magic or what?! Tell the story of the event here.

AFTERWORD

YOU'VE SPENT THE LAST TWO MONTHS TAKING CARE OF YOUR KITCHEN AND YOURSELF IN A NEW WAY. HOW DOES IT FEEL?

Aside from dry hands and broken nails, I bet good. The more you cook, the more you'll need to take care of your hands. Ditch nail polish, too. It will end up in your food! Invest in a few hand lotions to leave around the house, in your car and your handbags. My favorite nail kit comes from Bare Hands and my favorite hand lotion is a pale pink aluminum tube from Aesop.

Have any hand lotions you love?

If you have any cleaning up tips you want to add here, please write them down and share them! I'd love to hear your favorite dishwash soap or anything else related to keeping our kitchens, and selves, in magical shape.

ACKNOWLEDGEMENTS

I want to thank my parents for giving me the best of life. My dad, my friends Laura Winnick and Julie Podair, my sister-in-law Marie Christine Imbert and my brother-in-law Arul Thangavel, all of whom I consider the best cooks in my life.

My boyfriend and kindred spirit Steve, who was the first student of this no-recipe method. My godfather's husband Robert Jerome who edited the first iteration of this book and my editor Sara Lieberman who helped to format all my kitchen thinking into an eight-week journey. Thank you to Tracey Edelstein for providing counsel. Thank you to my incredible graphic designer Jena Richer who came in last minute and knew exactly what to do.

Thank you to all the people who have fed me over the years, from my mom who fed me from day one to Ella Greenberg who made the most garlicky, lemony broccoli of my childhood to Gizella Donald (Hungarian) and Theo Codrington (Caribbean). To Ezequiel Politzer whose sweet potatoes and chicken on Market Street in San Francisco were some of my favorite meals of all time. I love you all. And to all the many restaurants I've visited around the world, my thanks. I remember every one.

Photograph by Michael Rubin, 2020

ABOUT THE AUTHOR

Marguerite Imbert is a cultural critic, wellness guru and Internet personality. A graduate of Dartmouth College and a former writer for *The Michelin Guide*, Marguerite is also trained in physical and spiritual traditions—including as a yoga and meditation teacher, as well as a birth doula.

Marguerite is best known for her daily talk show on Instagram @margueritevimbert featuring world disruptors in all industries including food, fashion, art, beauty, and wellness. Raised in New York City, she is now based on the west coast, both in California and Washington. *Not a Cookbook* is her debut book.

NOT A COOKBOOK
© 2020 by Marguerite Imbert

All rights reserved. No part of this book may be used or reproduced in any official manner whatsoever without written permission from the author. Readers are free to photograph, quote and reference pages of the book at will on their own social media accounts, and author retains permission to repost at will.

Not A Cookbook can be purchased for educational, business, or sales promotional use. For information, please email stella@margueritevimbert.com

First published in 2020 by
Intuitive Noterie

ISBN 978-1-63684-810-5

Cover illustration by Alice Sutro
Interior illustrations by Marguerite Imbert
Book design by Jena Richer

Printed in USA
First printing 2020